FRONT COVER DESIGN AND INTERIOR ARTWORK
**BY BRANDY MARTIN**

# DEDICATION

"The hard thing that you are avoiding may be the greatest
gift that's ever happened to you."

-Monique Lecomte

# THE EXPERT
# GENERALIST

AN UNPAVED ROAD TO LEADERSHIP

MONIQUE LECOMTE

# FOREWORD

I always say that my childhood was robbed. By the time I was seven, I was the matriarch of our family. I cooked our meals, washed and hung our clothes, and ran errands like a grown woman trapped in a child's body. By age 12, I was driving a car. But more on that later.

My life started in a single-wide trailer on a red dirt road in the middle of nowhere, Alabama. Today, I train C-suite executives and other leaders around the world. I traded dirty, bare feet at the Winn-Dixie for high heels on the cobblestone streets of Europe and beyond— living proof that where you start does not determine where you finish.

The fact is, it's not the road that defines us. Our present and future are shaped by how we walk the long and ever-changing paths presented to us and how we can turn adversity into purpose.

Growing up in the 1970s, it was me, my mom, my brother, and my sister. A week into my baby sister's life, our dad left us in a town that the naked eye could not find on a map called Deatsville, Alabama. Or at least that's the story we were told.

We envisioned winning the Publishers Clearing House, playing every time it came in the mail. Then, we could upgrade to a double-wide trailer.

My mom used to say we were "poorer than poor." There are people who live near town and are barely getting by. And then, there are the people who are stranded in the country, 15+ miles from the nearest grocery store. We were the ones who were still skin and bones on government aid and welfare, scraping by in the backwoods of a town with less than 2,000 people.

And yet, somehow, I made it out. I made it out in a big way. My nearly 30-year career has led me to global boardrooms and leading teams for some of the most iconic brands.

When people hear my story today, they typically have the same question, expletive and all.

"How *the hell* did you get out?"

The pages that follow may give you a chuckle, a gasp, or a knowing nod as we follow along my journey through impossible odds to discover my escape route together.

The book you're holding offers a different perspective on success and leadership. I didn't go to business school. I didn't grow up with a dad. I didn't have a blueprint or even a role model. Yet, the lessons are the same as any successful businessperson. But instead of learning entrepreneurship on an Ivy League campus, my backdrop was hawking peaches in a K-Mart parking lot.

Looking back, it was inevitable that I would become The Expert Generalist. My upbringing was the ultimate lesson in sink or swim; there was no choice but to quickly become an expert in not just survival skills but also in resilience and creativity.

## EXPERT GENERALIST

*ex·pert /ek·sprt/*
*gen·er·al·ist /ˈjen-(uh)-ruh-list/*
*noun*
someone with a broad range of knowledge across disciplines. This enables them to connect ideas, solve complex problems, and easily adapt to challenges by drawing insights from varied perspectives.

My life was a blend of stark contrasts. With cinder blocks instead of stairs leading to the front door of our trailer, I grew up surrounded by the smell of the local paper mill mixed with toxic black fumes of burning tires from my Uncle Beanie's side hustle. Funny enough, the other smell was a sweet, earthy aroma from a six-foot-tall red rose bush—the only remnant from a grandmother I never knew.

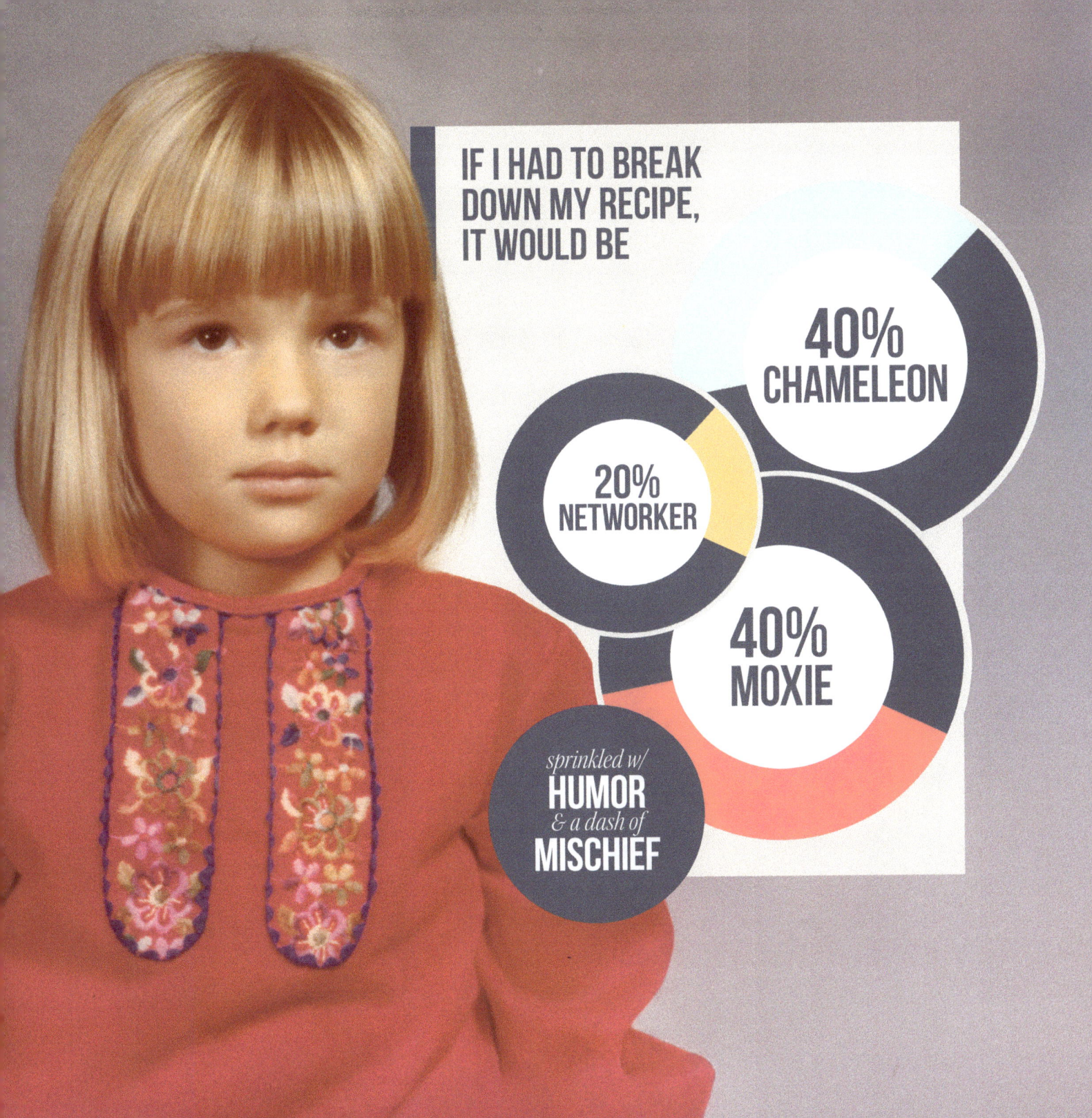

Do you remember your very first memory?

I was three years old. My mom was starting trade school in Montgomery. That first morning, she dropped my infant sister and me off at the free daycare on campus.

Back then, we were poster children for abject poverty in a place where over 60 percent of kids qualified for free lunch. The year I was born, over a quarter of the state lived below the poverty line, with a median family income of $9,265 per year. If you were one of the lucky ones that had a job, minimum wage was $1.60 an hour.

"Please don't leave me," I begged, clinging to her leg for dear life.

We had never been away from our mother at that point. She had been raising the

three of us on food stamps and welfare. This was her chance to make a better life for us.

A few days later, I ran into her in the bathroom of the small trade school.

"Are you here to save me?" a mix of whimpering and excitement in my unsteady voice. She looked like she'd seen a ghost and shook her head as she scuttled out of sight.

At age three, a theme that would set my life's trajectory had begun: no one is going to save you, except yourself.

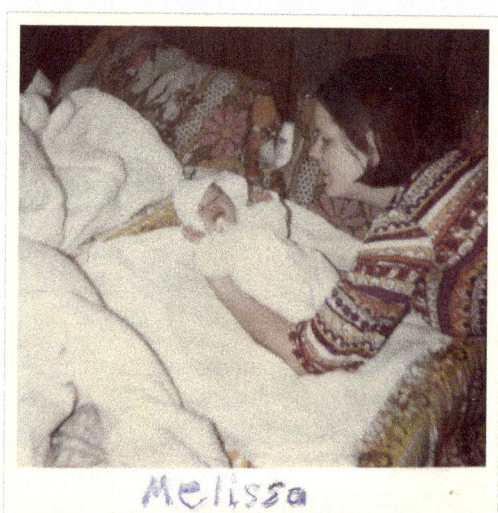

Melissa

For years, I hid the oppressive poverty of my childhood. Recently, I realized that resilience and 'overcoming' are too often missing from today's narrative on success. As it turns out, the hard thing you are avoiding may be the greatest thing that's ever happened to you.

My fundamental belief is that leadership isn't something you sign up for; it's something you step into. The obstacles we face, the friction and hardships we endure, and the choices we make define how we rise or fall. If we choose to be, we are *all* leaders.

Part of my story, captured in these short chapters, is an Aesop's Fables-inspired rendition of life lessons on determination, grit, and refusing to take "no" for an answer. Achieving in life is about seeing the inevitable detours as opportunities to push through and create new plan after new plan.

My hope for you is that you embrace the power of your own narrative and realize that no matter where you come from, you have the power to choose where you go.

In the Deep South, storytelling is as integral as sweet tea, serving both as a means to impart moral lessons and to entertain by recalling the past. These days, when everyone wants to "spill the tea," I still prefer to sip slowly in good company, savoring all the hard-won wisdom we can learn from each other.

*So grab a rocking chair and a glass of ice, and let me get the sun tea steeping for you.*

**SWEET HOME ALABAMA
WHERE THE SKIES ARE SO BLUE
SWEET HOME ALABAMA
LORD, I'M COMIN' HOME TO YOU**

*-Sweet Home Alabama by Lynyrd Skynyrd*

# CONTENTS

BACKSLIDERS & BLUE LAWS....01

LITTLE DEBBIES WITH LOUIS....02

THIS AIN'T COORS COUNTRY....03

PEACHES & THE PANHANDLE....04

THE POWER OF PLAY....05

THE CROSSROADS OF INJUSTICE....06

CROSSES & BULLHORNS....07

THE SNAKE SHOW....08

THE PERKS OF POVERTY....09

THE LOST PUPPY PICKER UPPERS....10

PLAYER'S CHOICE....11

4,201 MILES AWAY FROM HOME....12

ROAD TO NOWHERE....13

FOOD STAMPS AND FAIRYTALES....14

SALSA & SURVIVAL....15

THE GREAT EQUALIZER....16

FISH OUT OF WATER....17

CONTAGION....18

ROADMAPS & REVELATIONS....19

TOOT YOUR OWN HORN....20

RAIN CHECK....21

ALONE....22

FAMILY FIRST....23

SERVANT LEADERSHIP....24

THREE, TWO, ONE....25

BLACK SWAN....26

WWBD?....27

UNCLE ANDY + AUNT MO....28

TAKE IT EASY....29

REWILDIN'....30

# CHAPTER ONE

# AT THIS POINT, OUR LIFE WAS THE BIBLE.

## EVERYTHING REFLECTED BACK TO SCRIPTURE OR A PSALM.

# BACKSLIDERS & BLUE LAWS

I was always the youngest kid in my class. Technically, I started school at three years old. Soon after that whole bathroom ordeal with Mom, I started Kindergarten-4 at Grace Christian School at the local Baptist Church.

Starting school that early had a bigger impact on my life trajectory than anything else. Everywhere I went, from then on out, I was the youngest. To this day, I don't understand how the system allowed it. Maybe it was God's will.

School was sensory overload. I had never been around so many kids at the same time, kids of all skin colors and backgrounds. This was also my first experience of structure. We were wildlings at home—especially in the summer, roaming around the back hills with no adult supervision.

But at Grace Christian, there were rules and plenty of 'em. Girls were required to wear knee-length dresses, have long hair, and wear slips and stockings. Unlike the boys, we were not allowed to wear shorts, even under our dresses or during gym. It was basically Amish country without the bonnet.

# PERSONALITY TRAITS TO ENHANCE YOUR CHRISTIAN LIFE

When graduating K-5, we were all gifted the Christian Character Bible, Student Edition. The first few pages you won't find in the King James version. They were lined with bangers such as:

### SELF-CONTROL
bringing one's body under subjection through instant obedience to the Holy Spirit.

### OBEDIENCE
submission to God and those whom he puts in authority over me.

### PURITY
keeping yourself uncontaminated from the world, the flesh, and the Devil.

Grace Christian was my first introduction to Good vs. Bad. Hook, line, and sinker, I was a Believer. I would have dreams about smoking or doing bad things and wake up in a panic that I was going to Hell.

At this point, our life *was* the Bible. Everything reflected back to scripture or a psalm.

Rules dictated my early life. At school, it was the preacher's commanding presence. At home, it was Mom's relentless enforcement. In Alabama, it was the state's Blue Laws. These regulations banned anything other than worship on Sundays; stores were not open, people did not work, and you certainly weren't allowed to buy alcohol.

One day, a girl cut in line for the slide. I was so swept up in Right v. Wrong that my knee-jerk reaction was to yank her to the ground while yelling, "No Cuts!"

The gasps around me were immediate. Right had just become Wrong. Minutes later, I was in the head preacher's office, a scared five-year-old sitting across from someone who thought he was God himself. His booming voice made it clear where my actions would lead: straight to Hell. Tears flowed as I was sure my fate down under was sealed.

Toward the end of that school year, Mom left my 12-year-old brother in charge one afternoon as she sped off down our dusty one-lane road. Within minutes, she came stumbling back toward the trailer, blood streaking her face, and eyes wide with panic.

"I rolled the car," her voice trembled.

The wreck left us stranded for months. Town was too far to walk. With no wheels or other transportation nearby, we were isolated from the life we had known.

When we finally returned to church, eyes—who supposedly didn't judge others—followed us down the aisle. As the preacher announced the sermon for the day, he stared right at us.

"Backsliders," he thundered, "are those who turn away from God's grace."

I sat frozen in the pew, stealing glances at Mom. Her knuckles whitened around the Bible, her face unreadable except for a flicker of shame. On the way home, she barely spoke, her silence louder than the rumble of gravel.

Finally, she whispered, "We are finding a new church. And you girls are going to public school."

Suddenly, the rules changed.

*The Expert Generalist Lesson #1*
## ADAPTABILITY IS A SUPERPOWER

When you think something will be your foundation, it can shift at a moment's notice. Change in life is inevitable. What *is* fully under your control is whether you choose to embrace or resist it. You can either change your environment or change your mindset.

ONWARD, CHRISTIAN SOLDIERS,
MARCHING AS TO WAR,

WITH THE CROSS OF JESUS
GOING ON BEFORE!

CHRIST, THE ROYAL MASTER,
LEADS AGAINST THE FOE;

FORWARD INTO BATTLE, SEE HIS
BANNER GO!

-ONWARD, CHRISTIAN SOLDIERS

# CHAPTER TWO

# THERE IS A SAYING THAT GRIEF IS JUST LOVE WITH NOWHERE TO GO.

# LITTLE DEBBIES WITH LOUIS

By age seven, I knew and used every four-letter swear word in the book. I had traded my Bible for a public school Trapper Keeper, and there was no turning back.

Starting second grade at Prattville Primary was scary and exciting. The school bus became a rolling classroom, learning from kids aged five to nineteen. After being molded into the perfect pious follower, public school was my first experience as a rule-breaker. This would soon continue at home.

Enter: Afternoons with Granddaddy Louis.

Granddaddy was a towering figure, his thin frame wrapped in faded overalls that smelled faintly of engine grease and cigarettes.

Back in the day, Granddaddy was the gravity we orbited around. He'd bought three acres where Mom and my Aunt Dee had set up their trailers. My Uncle Beanie lived with him in a dark cabin on the property surrounded by Loblolly Pines.

I wonder to this day, if Granddaddy hadn't owned that land, *where would we have lived?*

His house was a refuge. It was the only place on the property cemented to the ground. We ran to Granddaddy's anytime there was a major storm or tornado coming through.

Being farthest from school, we were the kids who got picked up first and the last to get dropped off. After the 90-minute bus ride home, we'd run to the end of Granddaddy's driveway, just down the hill from our trailer.

"Y'all hungry?" he'd ask. *Did he know we hadn't eaten since our free lunch at 11:30am?*

His quiet presence filled the tiny log cabin. Granddaddy had stormed Normandy in World War II, but you'd never guess it from the way he moved through life—slow, deliberate, and impossibly calm.

His love didn't announce itself in grand gestures; it slipped into the small moments, like a package of Nutter Butters and Little Debbie cakes lined up with a glass of milk just for us. Granddaddy's soft chuckle filled the room as we tore into the wrappers like Christmas morning.

We'd settle onto the worn couch, crumbs pressed to our lips and cheeks, as *The Little Rascals* flickered in black and white on the old TV. It was our quiet haven, a bridge between the noise of school and the chaos waiting at home.

Mom never held a steady job for long. I remember her working at the gas station, stocking shelves at Walmart, and waiting tables. She ran a militant household, complete with yet another set of rules. Her #1 commandment: No sugar before dinner.

Come supper time, she'd yell from the top of the hill: "Stop giving those kids that sugar shit, Daddy!"

He'd grin, unbothered, and sneak us one more treat before sending us on our way, sticky-fingered and full of secrets.

I was nine when Granddaddy died. At first, I didn't shed a single tear. This stoicism was typical for me. Even at that age, my approach to emotion was: bury it.

Holding Mom's hand at the funeral, my chest felt like the Earth itself was pressing down on me. It was like I didn't know how to get the feelings out.

But then came the first shovel full of dirt onto the casket. The sharp, hollow sound cracked open my nine-year-old heart. The sobs spilled out, wild and unstoppable, as if I'd been holding back a lifetime of sorrow without realizing it.

It wasn't until years later that I realized how much we'd been left to soothe ourselves. Mom had her own grief and overwhelm to manage, which some would say came out in physical outbursts at our smallest missteps or mistakes. She had little room to teach us how to carry our emotions.

Even now, Nutter Butters are my favorite guilty pleasure—not just a cookie, but a small, sweet memory of the man who made us feel cared for without ever needing to say it.

Losing Granddaddy was more than losing our only father figure: it was losing the one constant in our ever-shifting world. His absence left a void for the rest of our lives. There is a saying that grief is just love with nowhere to go.

*The Expert Generalist Lesson #2*
## FEEL YOUR FEELINGS

Love doesn't always need words and grief doesn't either. If you stuff your feelings down (and distract, which is all too common today), they'll inevitably come up down the road in a way no amount of Nutter Butters can fix. Holding in emotions doesn't protect you; it harms you.

Bottom line: feel it to fix it.

SOME GLAD MORNING
WHEN THIS LIFE IS OVER

I'LL FLY AWAY

TO A HOME ON GOD'S
CELESTIAL SHORE

I'LL FLY AWAY

I'LL FLY AWAY, OH, GLORY

I'LL FLY AWAY

I'LL FLY AWAY

WHEN I DIE,
HALLELUJAH,

BY AND BY

I'LL FLY AWAY

-I'LL FLY AWAY
 BY ALBERT E. BRUMLEY

# CHAPTER THREE

The cashiers never hesitated to hand

# BEER & A PACK OF SMOKES

to us kids.

# THIS AIN'T COORS COUNTRY

In the Deep South, nearly everyone has a nickname. Mom was Suzy Q; her siblings were Beanie, Deeter, Bootie, and Janet.

Other than Granddaddy, Uncle Beanie was the most prominent man in my life. The baby brother of five, he never really grew up. He dropped out in sixth grade and Uncle Beanie's school of life became the misfits he surrounded himself with. After a failed marriage, he boomeranged back to my Granddaddy's house, which he soon inherited.

Uncle Beanie's crew was a staple on the family compound. Skeeter (my cousin with addiction issues), Trey and Ron (both truck drivers), Dick White (the town drunk), and dog after dog— always named "Man." Beanie's "Come Here, Man" never got old.

Another close friend of Beanie's was Boots Jackson. Like Beanie, Boots was your classic Southern drunkard, usually driving down the road while puffing on a cigarette in one hand and a cold Bud in the other. Ripped jeans and a stained white t-shirt were the uniform. Boots was the proud business owner of a not-so-aptly named honky-tonk called The Shangri-La.

For anyone who doesn't know (and oh, how I envy you), the dictionary defines a "honky-tonk" as follows:

## HONKY-TONK

*hon·ky-tonk /HAWNG-kee-tawnk/*
*noun*

a cheap or disreputable bar, club, or dance hall, typically where country music is played.

Half-lit, the bar itself was far from mythical but strangely magical. It was the place where adults went. No kids allowed.

Every weekend, Uncle Beanie and his drinking buddy Boots would concoct a plan to wrangle Tootie and Neekie (nicknames for my sister and me) into cleaning the entire bar for a whopping one hundred cents.

"Tootie! Neekie! Y'all wanna make some quarters today?" Uncle Beanie would holler up the hill. That was our intercom system, screaming up and down from our trailer to the cabin.

The Shangri-La represented doing something besides sitting on that dirt road. I could taste the forbidden fruits of Butterfingers and Coca-Cola already, which cost two quarters even. We could barely buy food, and Mom refused to spend our food stamps on anything besides staples like flour, Crisco, cornmeal, and butter beans.

Piling into the back of his red Chevy truck, Beanie'd take us down our dirt road to where the pavement started. Soon, we'd arrive in a gravel parking lot, littered with mini mountains of cigarette butts and Budweiser pop tops. Someone dumped the ashtrays out there daily, not even trying to hit a garbage can.

Stepping into The Shangri-La felt like a dank cave filled with ghosts from endless nights of bad decisions. The air was thick with stale beer, cigarette smoke, and sweat from the night before. Neon signs buzzed faintly on the walls, flickering. Hank Williams Senior played on repeat and Boots would be at his post, using a dirty rag to wipe down sticky counters layered with Jack and Coke.

At six and seven years old, the bar was our first taste of the grown-up world and my first paid job. We were expert cleaners already: scrubbing the trailer day and night, often getting a beating if things weren't just so.

"When I get back home, this place had better be clean," was Mom's classic threat.

I'd also sweep Granddaddy's cabin for quarters as often as possible. Beanie's friends usually sat there drinking as I wiped around their chairs like I was the entertainment.

From early on, I was a hustler, calculating how to make money indoors or outdoors. I would do anything above board for quarters and Coca-Cola: mowing lawns, raking pine straw, scouring bathrooms, etc.

Riding that public school bus was the first time I encountered kids with houses, nice clothes, and Trapper Keepers covered in the latest and greatest scratch and sniff stickers. Then and there, I knew we were poor and I wanted out.

Back at the Shangri-La, my assistant (Tootie) and I would climb on stools, elbows barely reaching the bar, and scrub away the syrupy grime. Pool tables at eye level became treasure hunts for loose change.

Our payday came in sticky coins, likely fished from the floor under the bar, but we didn't mind. A dollar in the early '80s was a goldmine to us.

*The Expert Generalist Lesson #3*
## HARD WORK NEVER HURT NO ONE

This was one of Mom's favorite mantras. Those who hustle can create their version of paradise, no matter the circumstances. Opportunity often disguises itself in hard work and unlikely places.

The next hustle became, "How many Cokes and candy bars can I buy in a week?"

We were soon running barefoot errands for Uncle Beanie and his drifter crew. Trips to the Hilltop store meant navigating a haze of secondhand smoke curling up from the painted faces and bright red lips of chain-smoking cashiers.

Our tasks were simple: fetch Marlboros (not those light ones), a six-pack of Bud, and pickled pig's feet. Uncle Beanie's Bible was quite the opposite of what we first learned at Grace Christian. It had just three commandments: Bud over Coors, Chevy over Ford, and Alabama football over Auburn.

The cashiers never hesitated to hand beer and a pack of smokes to us kids. All it took was a slurred call from Uncle Beanie—"Put it on my tab"— to seal the deal.

Boots Jackson's honky-tonk and its colorful cast are long gone, but the lessons remain. Some would say fitting: a local bought The Shangri-La a few years ago and turned it into a junkyard that still stands today.

WHEN YOU ARE SAD & LONELY &
HAVE NO PLACE TO GO

COME TO SEE ME, BABY,
& BRING ALONG SOME DOUGH

AND WE'LL GO HONKY TONKIN',
HONKY TONKIN'

HONKY TONKIN', HONEY BABY

WE'LL GO HONKY TONKIN' 'ROUND
THIS TOWN

-HONKY TONKIN' BY HANK WILLIAMS

# CHAPTER FOUR

SORRY, GEORGIA, BUT

# ALABAMA'S PEACHES ARE THE BEST

(ACCORDING TO MOM).

# PEACHES &
# THE PANHANDLE

W ho wants to sell some peaches so we can get to Florida?" Mike yelled from the yard, even though we didn't have a choice. Mike was Mom's latest loser boyfriend.

There are too many to remember, but Mike stood out. He seemed like one of the good ones. Maybe his friend Snake should've been the giveaway to his sleazy character. Theirs was a weird, drunk-buddy codependence, straight out of the Deep South central casting department.

Mike had a camper, and hatched a plan to fund a trip using us kids.

And so, at 10 years old, I unknowingly added another entrepreneurial role to my resume: selling peaches on a sunbaked truck hood.

The first stop was the Pick-Your-Own-Peach Farm in Chilton County—sorry Georgia, but Alabama's peaches are the best (according to Mom). At 95 cents a bushel, the markup potential had Mike's mouth watering.

Next, we posted up shop in the local K-mart parking lot. My sister and I leveraged our cuteness and my larger-than-life personality to attract customers in the blazing mid-July heat.

Who could resist two barefoot kids in shorts and smocked tops, hawking peaches with the charm only Southern children can muster?

Days of selling those peaches gave me a new perspective and a lifelong empathy for kids being used to make a buck. Even now, when I see them on the streets, I often stop to suss out the situation—offering food or toiletries instead of cash.

The money we made went straight to Mike. And that's just how it was. Mom didn't have a say. It was his plan, so it was his take.

My mother was a magnet for these kinds of men. They could smell her from a mile away, like stank on shit (pardon my French, but it's important you get an authentic taste of Southern vernacular). People would ride roughshod over her. Mike was just the latest parasite.

WHO COULD RESIST **TWO BAREFOOT KIDS IN SHORTS AND SMOCKED TOPS, HAWKING PEACHES WITH** THE CHARM ONLY SOUTHERN CHILDREN **CAN MUSTER?**

PEACHES FOR SALE

The trip to Florida itself was forgettable. I don't even remember going to the beach. We rode in Mike's truckbed camper with no air conditioning or bathroom. There were the five of us (including Mike's buddy, the ever-blacked-out Snake, of course) sleeping in that roaster box.

We drove through the night and parked. In the morning, we opened the camper door to our first sight in Florida, a sign reading:

We shut the door tight. Any time we snuck in a burst of wet Panhandle air, Mom would scream, "Y'all be careful out there and make sure you're not up to your ass in alligators."

Soon after we got home, the revolving door of boyfriends swung open and shut again. One after another, predators fixin' to use a single mother of three and her kids any way they could. Give 'em an inch and you might just end up in Florida by morning.

*The Expert Generalist Lesson #4*
## DON'T FEED THE ALLIGATORS

Effort without boundaries invites exploitation. Constantly giving to those who only take will leave you drained. Recognize the difference between collaboration and being used. Protect your time, your work, and your worth. If you keep feeding the takers, they'll keep coming back for more.

# CHAPTER FIVE

Play wasn't handed to us; **WE INVENTED IT.**

# THE POWER OF PLAY

**M**om didn't go looking for solace in the summers; she created it. She wasn't about to share the single-wide with three kids, night *and* day.

Come sun up, we were given the boot. Locked out of the trailer, we looked after ourselves til supper. Raising kids was different back then. The approach was basically: *You're a kid, go play. See you at dinner.*

Our days were a patchwork of manual labor and adventure. We rushed through our list of chores, fast as we could, to get to the 'wildling' portion of our summer days.

In the mornings, we'd spend hours in Mom's garden, digging up potatoes, and shelling purple hull peas til our fingers tinted violet. Daily list done, we'd collapse in the shade, watermelon juice dripping from our chins and the rusty rubber taste of garden hose water on our tongues.

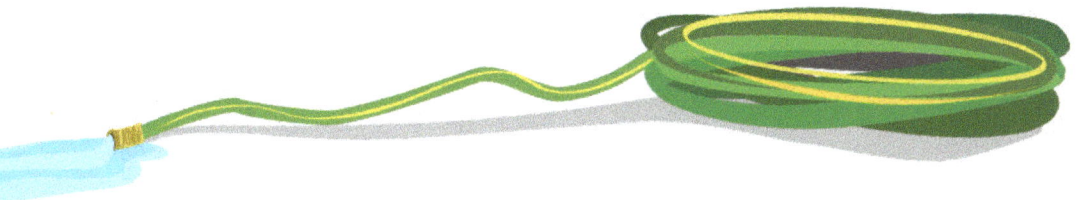

But hard work wasn't the only thing that shaped us. The play did, too.

We didn't have many store-bought toys. This lack inspired a near-endless spring of courage and enough reckless creativity to turn our neck of the woods and some trash into the best playground we'd ever known.

*"Ready, set, GO!"* one of us would shout as we launched down the hill onto homemade potato sack sleds. The ground slipped away behind us as we skidded toward the dirt road, laughter mixing with the scrape of burlap against the pine straw.

Everything became a game.

"Bet you won't hit the edge!" we'd taunt, daring gravity to hurl us farther.

"Y'all trying to kill yourselves?" Mom's voice would blare out the window of her '64 Chevy as we dove headfirst into the woods, trying to escape her sporadic check-ins. Heart pounding and fingers crossed behind our backs, we'd promise to keep away from the road. But the thrill of the next dare pumped louder.

There's an energy kids unlock when left to their own devices—a mix of primal instinct and feral free-for-all. One summer, we unearthed the ultimate wild kid's treasure: a rusted-out go-kart buried in a friend's yard. The frame was wrapped in kudzu vines and the cushion seat barely clung together with duct tape.

"It doesn't need gas!" I declared.

From a young age, I naturally stepped up as the ringleader, instinctively leaning into my knack for leadership.

Sweat was soon dripping down our faces as we dragged the newfound prize up the hill. Its wheels wobbled and the steering was shot, but with no one to assess the safety of the situation, the next step was inevitable.

"Hold on tight!" I yelled, as I gave the kart a running launch.

Off it went, careening down the hill, bouncing over rocks, driver gripping the wheel for dear life. Screams of laughter echoed through the trees as we lined up to see who could coast the farthest.

Play wasn't handed to us; we invented it. This seems all too uncommon these days—when kids' eyes aren't even allowed to wander, glued to a screen as their only form of "adventure."

Years later, when I was 42, I played tennis for the first time. Someone asked why I hadn't learned earlier in life. I nearly spit out my coffee. *Courts? Clubs? You had to have money for those.*

Looking back, I realize my childhood was a master's degree in leadership, bravery, and improv. Every skid down the hill, every flip off a branch, and every sprint from trouble drew a blueprint for ingenuity.

And that approach to life? It sticks with you long after the bruises fade.

*The Expert Generalist Lesson #5*
## CREATE YOUR OWN PLAYBOOK

Your brain is the best supercomputer. When the world doesn't hand you an instruction manual (or anything to play with), use your imagination to create the reality you want to see. Making your own playbook doesn't just leave you with memories—it leaves you with a mindset.

Instead of looking it up, give yourself a shot!

# CHAPTER SIX

# THE WHIRRING FANS DID LITTLE MORE THAN STIR THE HUMID AIR.

# THE CROSSROADS OF INJUSTICE

Turn the car around!" I cried from Uncle Beanie's truck bed. Our backsides were scalding on the metal, but it wasn't the oppressive heat that had us on edge.

It was the KKK. Yep, that KKK. Thumb out, a towering man in homemade sheetwear wanted to hop in back with us kids as we passed through Selma.

White robe and pointy hood, he represented faceless racism at its finest. Proud for all the wrong reasons, like the original Proud Boys auditioning for a hate parade.

Uncle Beanie didn't even tap the brakes. If anything, he pressed the gas like he was qualifying for Talladega.

In those summer months, our two-bedroom trailer became a pressure cooker where four people had no choice but to coexist. The whirring fans did little more than stir the humid air. Chiggers—those invisible, maddening harvest mites—made the woods a battlefield, leaving trails of fiery red welts on our ankles. Scratching made it worse.

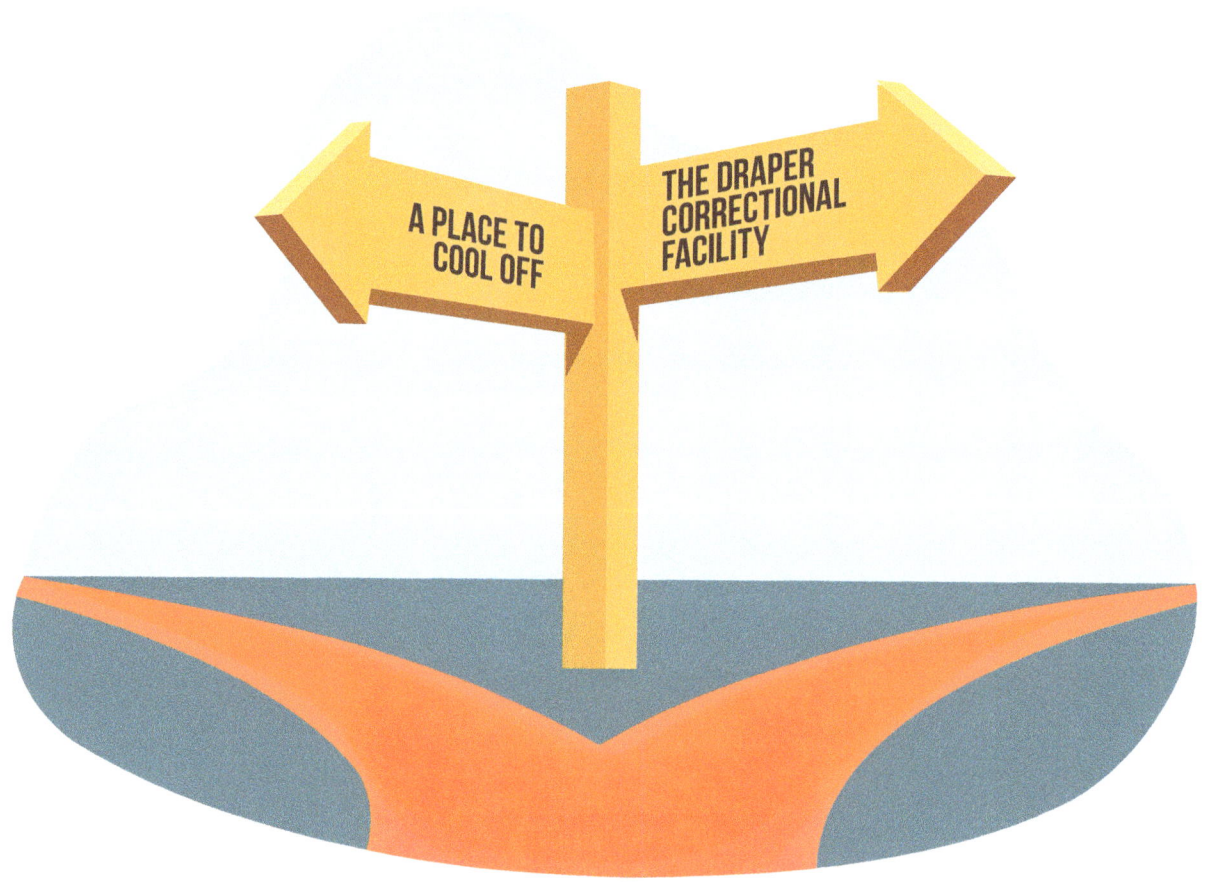

Mom was usually home, whether she was out of work or escaping life by watching her "soaps." Beanie spent the days rebuilding the latest manual engine of a Chevy, pounding back a 12-pack of Bud.

Relief from the heat was hard to find, so it was something we hunted. More days than not, we set off on our classic summer search for swimming holes at Speigner Lake, Cooter's Pond, Froggy Bottom Pond, and on and on. We called them "lakes," though most were nothing more than muddy pits.

Driving on the road to Speigner Lake was a paradox in itself: turn left and you found a place to cool off, turn right and you ended up at the Draper Correctional Facility.

Further down AL-143, we could expect a familiar sight every time: white men on horseback with 12-gauge rifles marching mostly Black prisoners (called "chain gangs") to the cotton and corn fields. Wearing leg irons and shackled at the wrists, the men labored away in fields, sometimes for 12 scorching hot hours.

Even as kids, we knew this wasn't right. It was the 1980s, but may well have been the 1860s.

Terror lingered in the South and not just from the open presence of the KKK. The last recorded lynching in the United States was still hot in the air. In 1981, 19-year-old Michael

Donald was kidnapped and murdered by two Klan members in Mobile, Alabama. The lawsuit that followed bankrupted the Klan nationwide, but couldn't erase the stain they'd left behind.

It may have different villains and heroes, but make no mistake: history always repeats itself.

*The Expert Generalist Lesson #6*
## MORAL CLARITY MATTERS

When we live with a foundation of integrity and morals, the compass is clear. Right is right, and wrong is wrong. Regardless of our politics or religion, we can all do better.

*One action you can take is to support organizations like the **Equal Justice Initiative**, a nonprofit in Montgomery. Founded in 1989 by **Bryan Stevenson**, a renowned public interest lawyer and social justice advocate. EJI is dedicated to challenging racial and economic injustice, ending mass incarceration and excessive punishment in the United States, and protecting fundamental human rights for the most vulnerable. Visit **www.eji.org** to learn more.*

# CHAPTER SEVEN

# SINNERS, REPENT!

## or suffer the wrath of

# ETERNAL DAMNATION

# CROSSES & BULLHORNS

Sinners, REPENT! Or suffer the wrath of eternal damnation," boomed through a garbled bullhorn from a beat-down truck filled with fire-and-brimstone crosses.

W.C. Rice had just driven by in downtown Prattville (the "big city" nearest to Deatsville).

If you wanted to scare kids in town, you didn't need haunted houses or ghost stories when you had W.C. Rice. In my hometown, he was both legend and nightmare, spewing warnings of damnation and words of salvation to anyone who'd listen (or couldn't avoid it).

His yard, famously dubbed "The Cross Garden," was a chaotic, mentally unwell monument to fear and faith, plastered with messages of repentance—or else. Some might call it folk art, but it felt like a Southern Gothic graveyard come to life.

When we weren't inundated with the blaring of W.C., the sound of certain music would get us in trouble.

All six churches we'd gone to set off the alarm bells for the "Satanic Panic." According to them: all rock music was Devil music.

Despite each church's best efforts, music was our lifeline. One morning, while searching for treasure in the rusted-out cars and trucks dotting Uncle Beanie's front yard, we struck gold.

We were mesmerized when we inserted the tape into my mini boombox & hit play.

"Don't you dare be listenin' to that Devil music!" Mom snapped.

Led Zeppelin was not on the approved list. Other than the Eagles and a few other bands Mom let slip through, the soundtrack to our days was mostly *The 700 Club* (still running today) with Pat Robertson, and Jim and Tammy Faye Bakker's *Praise The Lord Club*.

"Our prayer team will pray for every request [if you send us your money]," the scripted words would hang heavy with practiced sincerity. These spectacles unfolded with stories of faith, world news spun through a Christian lens, and, of course, the familiar plea for donations.

THERE'S A LADY WHO'S SURE ALL THAT GLITTERS IS GOLD

AND SHE'S BUYING A STAIRWAY TO HEAVEN WHEN SHE GETS

THERE SHE KNOWS, IF THE STORES ARE ALL CLOSED

WITH A WORD SHE CAN GET WHAT SHE CAME FOR

OOH OOH & SHE'S BUYING A STAIRWAY TO HEAVEN

-STAIRWAY TO HEAVEN BY LED ZEPPELIN

The hypocrisy was glaring—both Pat Robertson and the Bakkers amassed hundreds of millions of tax-free dollars under the guise of tithing for the Lord, endlessly asking for more from those who could barely make ends meet. Somehow, their cup never runneth over enough to share with their flock.

We also had traveling preachers come through town, making their money by hosting "Revivals." These hoaxsters brought live snakes to sell their oil: "Come to the front TODAY to be saved and not spend eternity in Hell." Dozens would fall to their knees, speaking in tongues and babbling utter nonsense. So it must've worked.

Around the same time, Prattville had another character who took an alternate approach to spreading the gospel. He'd outdo himself every year with an over-the-top display of Christmas lights. What started as a few decorations on his trailer soon spread across his yard like kudzu, each year bigger and brighter, until it resembled something out of "National Lampoon's Christmas Vacation"—but ten times more intense. His display didn't shout warnings of doom; instead inviting joy, connection, and a shared sense of wonder in a town that often felt small and predictable.

These Believers, opposites in delivery of their love for Jesus, embodied the quirks and contradictions of the Deep South. W.C. Rice and the traveling preachers used fear as the tool, broadcasting condemnation and judgment. The Christmas light enthusiast used festivity and hope to draw people together.

Prattville's eccentric evangelicals, whether preaching Hellfire or stringing up lights, taught me that the method matters.

*The Expert Generalist Lesson #7*
## LEAD WITH KINDNESS

Words carry weight, and how we deliver them determines whether we build or burn bridges. Intimidation may get attention but this approach doesn't earn trust or connection. Ultimately, what matters isn't just the message but how you make people feel when you share it.

Be the voice people lean into, not one they turn away from.

# CHAPTER EIGHT

# WHOOPS!

the snake handler
shrugged as the
King Cobra fell five
feet from our faces.

# THE SNAKE SHOW

Santa Claus of the Reptile Kingdom stood on stage behind his table, pulling snakes out of his bag straight out of a scene from Tiger King.

A source of education for us kids, the reptile handler would start by presenting the harmless garden snake and progress up the poisonous ladder from there. I remember them being stored in pillowcases. The rattling and hissing sounds will never leave me.

"Whoops!" the snake handler shrugged, as his King Cobra fell five feet from our faces. Cue 100+ kids screaming at his classic fake-out trick.

For a split second that felt like a lifetime, I thought this was The End. Trembling and terrorized, I bolted back to my classroom with tears streaming down my cheeks.

The Snake Show was supposed to teach us how to stay safe in the South, where 50-60 species of venomous and non-venomous snakes enjoy the hot and humid climate. But *my* biggest takeaway was a lifelong fear of snakes, literally and metaphorically.

In those days, spring season included school photos that were full-on productions, complete with hired entertainment.

My fondest memory of class photos was in the second grade. The theme was Cowboys. Back then, we played 'Cowboys and Indians' without a second thought—a game shaped by the times, before we understood the deeper history behind it.

During our first year of public school, Mom wanted to shake our image as the raggedy kids who only survived on handouts. She pinched pennies and cut corners on food for weeks until we finally saved enough for my dream outfit: a red-and-white checkered shirt with fringe, matching pants, and a pair of brown boots that clicked with every step.

Mom cut a deal with the owner of the local western wear shop. When she brought home the paper bag from Kohn's Western Mall, I knew the time had finally come. I slid into the outfit like a Dallas Cowboy cheerleader getting ready for game day, grinning as I admired myself in the mirror.

ON THAT DAY IN 1981, I LIVED MY DREAM OF BEING A TRUE COWGIRL. I STOOD TALL, COWBOY HAT IN HAND, READY FOR MY CLOSE-UP.

That outfit became my identity. I wore it until the boots were too much to bear in the heat, and the pants were cut into shorts. I kept the cowgirl spirit alive, racing barefoot through the woods.

Growing up, we either had layaway clothes only at the start of the school year or ones sewed by Aunt Janet. So I knew that outfit was a sacrifice for Mom and it was a badge of honor for me.

## But snakes? *They were a different story.*

My least fond memory of school photo season was that scary Snake Show in the fifth grade, planting a seed in me that I am still all too aware of today.

For many years, snakes were a recurring theme in my life. They lurked in the fun places of my childhood: creek beds, swimming holes, and the ditches we played in.

"Watch out for water moccasins," Mom would warn us. Cottonmouth snakes can be deadly and love hanging out in—you guessed it—water!

The spring after the King Cobra incident, I refused to pay the $1 entry fee to that year's Snake Show.

Hiding alone in the safety of my classroom, I watched the door like a vigilante cowgirl. NO SNAKES allowed.

*The Expert Generalist Lesson #8*
### KNOW WHEN TO WALK AWAY

Courage doesn't only mean facing what scares you; it can also be the act of recognizing your personal limits and enforcing boundaries around them—at any age.

YOU'VE GOT TO KNOW WHEN TO HOLD 'EM

KNOW WHEN TO FOLD 'EM

YOU'VE GOT TO KNOW WHEN TO WALK AWAY

KNOW WHEN TO RUN

YOU NEVER COUNT YOUR MONEY

WHEN YOU'RE SITTIN' AT THE TABLE

THERE'LL BE TIME ENOUGH FOR COUNTIN'

WHEN THE DEALIN'S DONE

-THE GAMBLER BY KENNY ROGERS

"cain't never could."

# THE PERKS OF POVERTY

One sticky Alabama summer when I was 11 and my sister was 10, our unsupervised playtime ended abruptly.

The lukewarm pools of the local YMCA and its concrete complex replaced our endless woods. The locker rooms reeked of Lysol, sweat, and humidity, but they were perfect greenhouse for fun and occasional mold.

This new summer routine became my idea of heaven. Welfare checks and food stamps kept our bellies full, but the YMCA gave us something more: the freedom to feel like regular kids. Day camps and after-school programs were our ticket to a world where possibility replaced poverty the moment we walked through the front doors.

Like many kids in our town, we relied on government aid and non-profits. Back then, nearly 25 percent of Alabama's population lived in poverty. Sadly, little has changed. As of 2024, Alabama is the seventh poorest state in the nation (according to the U.S. Census Bureau).

At school, our free-lunch card mixed with our hand-me-down outfits to make us a mark and easy prey for bullying and judging whispers.

But at the YMCA, we all ate the same sandwich and apple. Our red and blue camp t-shirts leveled the playing field. It didn't matter how much (or little) our parents made, we were all day campers. No one had to know that we also got free swim lessons.

Swimming—or more specifically, drowning—was basically my biggest fear. No one in my family could swim, which made trips to the swimming hole all the more chancey.

"I cain't," my sister and I would whine.

"But you haven't even tried yet. How do you know you cain't?" Mom would retort back. "Cain't never could."

For those that need translation: this saying is considered Southern folk wisdom, passed down, mostly among parents and elders. It was our take on "If you don't try, you'll never know."

Two weeks after our first time ever stepping foot into a pool, there we stood in a line of kids inching toward the deep end. It was time for the ultimate test: jumping off the diving board to get the coveted Minnow Badge.

I tiptoed to the edge when it was my turn and the swim instructor hollered, "JUMP!"

In I went, in what onlookers might've called a shaky trust fall forward.

My Badge became a symbol of courage and confidence. I had done it; overcome my fear.

I didn't stop there—I learned freestyle, backstroke, and breaststroke, each new skill a step further from "I cain't" to "I can."

The adventure that summer continued: the YMCA hosted overnight lock-ins and field trips, complete with plenty of "unholy music." We were introduced to lyrics that felt downright rebellious.

The YMCA wasn't just a place—it was a launchpad. It took kids weighed down by a never-ending "we can't afford that," and inspired us to believe that scarcity didn't define us.

*The Expert Generalist Lesson #9*
## JUMP INTO THE DEEP

Life is full of complete unknowns. There's no way around it. Getting comfortable with confidently stepping out of your comfort zone is a practice, just like yoga or lifting weights. Proving to yourself that you are capable of navigating life's challenges only happens when you do it over and over. When we dare to leap into the deep, we often discover we're capable of more than we ever imagined.

Turns out, Mom was right all along: "Cain't never could."

# DRIVING THAT TRAIN, HIGH ON COCAINE. CASEY JONES, YOU BETTER WATCH YOUR SPEED. TROUBLE AHEAD TROUBLE BEHIND AND YOU KNOW, THAT NOTION JUST CROSSED MY MIND.

- The Grateful Dead

# CHAPTER TEN

# THE LOST PUPPY PICKER UPPERS

L iving in the boondocks meant we didn't have proper garbage service. Out there in the middle of nowhere, the nearest option was a perpetually-overflowing dumpster that happened to be right down the road from our trailer.

Picture this: a renegade landfill surrounded by broken sofas, air conditioners with freon leaking out, random car parts, old mattresses, and who knows what else? It was a scene straight out of Mad Max Beyond Thunderdome.

The majority of people offloading trash didn't live nearby and the discarding itself wasn't limited to stuff. Sadly enough, drive-by dog and cat dumps were more common than not.

Usually, they were mangy, sick animals infested with ticks and fleas. Mom's giving heart meant that she would apply God's care to each creature in need. My sister and I would be the ones to apply the Kreso dip. We'd smell like coal tar and antiseptic for days after each treatment.

Once, my sister convinced Mom to add another orphan dog to our pack after we watched her (who we later named Brownie) trying to retrieve a dead puppy from her litter on the side of the road.

You would've thought that our trailer was Noah's Ark. But it wasn't just two by two; it was car after car of stray puppies, kittens, dogs, and cats. Despite our struggles, we took in nearly every one of them, feeding them scraps and offering unconditional love. They'd stay a while, then disappear, only to be replaced by new strays.

In an act straight out of the Book of Genesis, Mom picked up the slack, giving more than she had. Without a word about it, she taught us to give unconditionally simply by modeling the way.

**MOM'S** GIVING HEART **MEANT THAT SHE WOULD APPLY GOD'S CARE TO EACH** CREATURE IN NEED.

# ALWAYS HAVE A GIVER'S HEART

The true power of giving lies in expecting nothing in return, not even a photo for social media. This principle applies to both life and leadership: lend a hand when you are in a position to—or even when you're not.

In a world obsessed with recognition, why does kindness have to be an occasion?

# CHAPTER ELEVEN

WE HAD JUST GOTTEN A NEW DRYER, OUR FIRST. BEFORE THEN,

WE'D SPEND HOURS PINNING OUR CLOTHES AND SHEETS TO THE LINE OUTSIDE.

# PLAYER'S CHOICE

G o pick your switch," Mom barked through the chorus of hysterical crying. My heart sank as I trudged toward the Mimosa tree, not only from the impending sting but from the anger of knowing this was wrong.

Picking the correct switch was an art—too thin, and it stung like a swarm of bees, bloodying your legs and backside; too thick, and it thudded, leaving bruises that lingered. I walked past Grandma's roses toward my perfect switch bush.

In the Deep South, getting switched was as common as checking the mail six days a week. Alabama law permits it. As recently as 2018, over 30 percent of schools in Alabama reported using corporal punishment. Unbelievable, when you think about it...

That day, we were playing a soon-to-be infamous hide-and-seek game when I decided to take it up a notch. We had just gotten our very first dryer. Before then, we'd spend hours pinning our clothes and sheets to the line outside.

The appliance was the perfect hiding spot. That is, until I shifted too much weight onto the door and *crunnnnch!* The metal broke from its hinge. I froze, heart pounding but not stopping the game for a second. Determination ruled the day and I was not a loser.

Moments later, I heard our mother screaming. "Who the fuck broke the dryer door? 'Cause you're about to get your ass beat."

I had gone too far this time. My brother, sister, and I scattered like squirrels into the woods. By the time Mom found us, she was livid.

"Who did it?" she demanded, looking from one ashen face to the next. I stayed silent.

Soon, my stomach was twisting as the switch lashed against my siblings' bare legs. Their yelps bit into my conscience, knowing I could have spared them. Mom's hard work and paychecks were gone in a single crunch, and we all paid for it with welts on our legs.

That would not be the first or last time we got a switching.

Those moments etched deep into who I became, forcing me to build walls around my emotions. They felt like a weakness I couldn't afford.

Looking back, those moments were more than just punishment—they were the language of fear, survival, and a mother overwhelmed by the weight of raising three kids on her own.

## AS A TEENAGER, RESENTMENT TOWARD MOM BURNED HOT, ESPECIALLY WHEN THE SWITCH CAME DOWN.

At the time, switch felt like an injustice I couldn't escape, but now I see it for what it was: her desperate attempt to protect us from a world she couldn't control. She was parenting based on the only way she knew: her own lived experience.

With time and distance, my anger faded, replaced by a quiet understanding. I can only imagine how lonely and burdened she must have felt, with no one to fall back on in good times or bad.

To be clear, I don't condone beating children, under ANY circumstance, even in the 17 states where it's currently legal(!). But if I could go back, I'd hug my mother and tell her I understand and that maybe, just maybe, we were both doing the best we could with the little that we had.

The welts faded every time, but lessons about the complicated love that shaped my childhood remain. I've learned to hold both truths: the harm of those moments and the humanity behind them.

*The Expert Generalist Lesson #11*
## GIVE GRACE

Life ain't easy. Many times people are doing the best they can or the best they know how. They may be going through some invisible battle that others will never see. Instead of looking for places to be upset when people inevitably mess up (just like we all do), look for understanding.

What if we made it our daily practice to simply Give Grace?

# CHAPTER TWELVE

"WE'RE GOING TO MOVE TO ALASKA WITH YOUR FATHER. **START FRESH.**"

# 4,201 MILES FROM HOME

**M**y sister stood beside me, her eyes darting nervously between the stalls and the door of the Montgomery Airport bathroom.

I could hear her swallow hard before she whispered, "I'm scared."

My stomach churned, a sick knot tightening. I nodded, overcome by an unusual silence.

We were about to meet him—*the stranger*. The man who left us in Alabama all those years ago. I was one when my father walked out, too young to remember his face. Now, at 12, that emptiness had a shape and it stood waiting just outside.

"We're going to move to Alaska with your father. Start fresh."

Mom had sold us on the idea like it was some sort of family reunion tour.

Her latest plan was to trade red dirt roads and sweltering heat for icy wilderness and permafrost. Our father, who was having a mid-life crisis after his third failed marriage, must've thought this was his ticket to redemption.

And so, that was that. In a flash, over winter break and without the chance to say goodbye to friends, we were packed into a handful of suitcases and about to get on a plane for the first time.

Fear of heights in the back of my throat, there was no time for that. The life I knew was about to be 4,201 miles in the rearview. By the third connecting flight, I was a pro. Using that hard-earned superpower of adaptability, I had accepted my fate.

Winter knocked the wind slap out of us. The air bit at our noses and cheeks, so cold it burned. We had no concept of freezing, much less 20 below. The smell of sulfur and diesel was a cocktail that brings me back to Alaska even now.

I tried to match Mom's forced optimism, even though the weight in my chest wouldn't lift.

*This is home now*, I repeated silently to myself.

Fairbanks wasn't just far—it was another planet. Gone were our beloved Loblolly Pines, replaced by snow forests called "taiga" that I'd only seen in the encyclopedias at school.

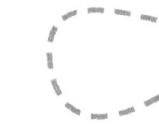

# STARS IN OUR EYES, OUR DREAM OF A DOUBLE-WIDE TRAILER WAS SUDDENLY ECLIPSED BY A TWO-STORY HOUSE.

Alaska itself was a land of firsts. Not only was it my first time seeing snow and mountains, but I'd never lived in a neighborhood right next door to other houses and families that weren't our own. We swapped the full bed that my sister and I shared for our very own bedrooms. We weren't used to living somewhere we could walk everywhere, let alone anywhere.

New friends, new adventures, new (old) father. Alaska, known as the last frontier, was my first experience of pioneering a new life out West.

Everything was a great unknown.

*Would people ever understand our (very) country accents? Was our family finally going to be whole? Or was this just another of Mom's delusions that we would be saved?*

This may not be a surprise to you, but our simple Southern Baptist mother was unable to reconcile with our narcissistic atheist dad. Leopards don't change their spots.

Just as quickly as we had migrated north, we flew back south. Sharing a bed with my sister again (which we did for 16 years) and back in our trailer in the boonies, a lightbulb switched on: life can just change. At Mach speed.

My life had changed more in six months than it had in my first 12 years. Alaska left its mark and showed me that sometimes, life's decisions are made for you.

After four months, she left us with him. Yep, you read that right.

Soon after, he too was done with the big house and the acting part of Dad in a nuclear family. Off to our newest new digs—a soon-to-be bachelor pad that was still bigger than our hillside mobile home. The school year in Alaska ended and...

POOF.

As if it had never happened, we were back at the Montgomery Airport.

*The Expert Generalist Lesson #12*
## CONTROL WHAT YOU CAN

Life rarely goes as planned—sometimes you're uprooted, forced to start over, or watching things fall apart. When life serves you the unexpected, lean in, learn from it, and adjust accordingly. Make the choice to make do with what you've got, and you are likely to discover resilience, growth, and even joy in any situation.

# CHAPTER THIRTEEN

GO TO CHURCH or the DEVIL WILL GET YOU!

# ROAD TO NOWHERE

While Mom was hogging the TV and glued to her soaps, I often found myself perched on an overpass down the hill from our house, watching silent voyagers roll underneath. The hum of I-65 was my entertainment. I waved at the semis roaring by, wondering: *Will they honk?* And the bigger question: *Where are all these people going?*

My sister and I first heard stories of the open road at Uncle Beanie's. The men in my family were natural galavanters. From hitchhiking cousins with cardboard signs that read "B-HAM or BUST"...to Uncle Jerry, who was a career truck driver...to Cousin Mark, who joined the Army to travel the world (and get out of Dodge).

We would listen through secondhand smoke while sitting on mismatched chairs and a dirty sofa.

Each of their stories further fueled my desire to

explore life outside Prattville. While my aunts would talk about everything and nothing—basically limited to who was getting married, had a baby, or died—the men's conversations felt simple, rugged, and full of wonder. I hung on every word, hearing things I probably shouldn't have.

I-65 stretches all the way from the Great Lakes to the Gulf of Mexico and always fascinated me, a lifeline to something bigger than our small town. We got glimpses of trucker life from the stragglers who hung out at Uncle Beanie's between runs too. We'd spend hours playing with CB radios, chatting, and dreaming of distant lands.

Sometimes, Mom would drive us North to visit Aunt Mattie. Those short trips often turned into traveling sermons. Just past a familiar curve, we'd see a hand-painted sign near a water wheel declaring, "Go to Church or the Devil Will Get You!"

# "SEE THAT? THAT'S WHY WE GO TO CHURCH EVERY WEDNESDAY AND SUNDAY. YOU BETTER BE GOOD GIRLS!"

Mom would seize the moment, jabbing a finger toward the window.

"See that? That's why we go to church every Wednesday and Sunday. You better be good girls!" she hollered into the backseat, her voice filled with the triumph of a Believer's heart.

Decades later, the paint might be peeling, but the ominous message still clings to those very billboards, like it's doing God's work (or maybe the Devil's). Heaven and Hell bled into every corner of our lives—music, school, family rules, and more.

In retrospect, the irony of it all wasn't lost on me. The songs we weren't supposed to hear, the VHS tapes we weren't supposed to watch, and even the forts we built to escape felt like rebellion. Maybe it wasn't rebellion at all. Maybe it was survival.

SHOUT, SHOUT, SHOUT!

SHOUT AT THE DEVIL!

SHOUT, SHOUT, SHOUT!

"Shout at the Devil" by Motley Crue

These days, the first notes of the song "Shout at the Devil" by Motley Crue make me grin. Every time I hear it now, I'm reminded of that spark of mischief we all carry within.

If my sister and I weren't in church pews on any given Sunday, we were looking out the window of an 18-wheeler's weed-infused cab. Probably thrilled to have a brief slice of silence, Mom didn't seem to mind when we climbed into trucks with grizzled 40-year-olds.

This exposure to different people and places ignited a lifelong passion for exploration and untamed landscapes—forever curious about what lies beyond the horizon. The great outdoors and a good road trip continue to be my mobile sanctuary, but the Devil no longer rides shotgun.

*The Expert Generalist Lesson #13*
## BE CURIOUS

Every question we ask, every perspective we seek, and every road we're willing to explore can lead to breakthroughs we never imagined. New people, ideas, and situations might not seem connected at first, but very often end up turning into something extraordinary.

YOU GOT IT
ROLL ON HIGHWAY,
ROLL ON ALONG
ROLL ON, DADDY, 'TIL
YOU GET BACK HOME

ROLL ON FAMILY,
ROLL ON CREW
ROLL ON, MAMA, LIKE
I ASKED YOU TO DO &
ROLL ON, EIGHTEEN-WHEELER,
ROLL ON

-ROLL ON (EIGHTEEN WHEELER) BY ALABAMA

# CHAPTER FOURTEEN

# WE LIVED A CONTROLLED CHILDHOOD—

### TIGHT BUDGETS, TIGHT RULES, AND EVEN TIGHTER LIVING QUARTERS.

# FOOD STAMPS & FAIRYTALES

The wheels of Mom's Renault Alliance crunched across the rocks and pine straw of our driveway as my sister and I pushed the car, one inch at a time.

We lived a controlled childhood—tight budgets, tight rules, and even tighter living quarters. Whether it was by bicycle, go-kart, or my neighbor's four-wheeler, I figured out early that wheels can take you a lot farther from home than bare feet.

The bright idea to steal Mom's car came to me at age 12, after yet another "no" to my endless begging to learn how to drive. I'd hawk-eyed her enough times that I decided I could figure a stick shift out myself.

Mom was still quiet in bed, worn out from late nights waiting tables. I slipped her ring of keys quietly off their hook and off Tootie and I went.

As usual, we were raising ourselves, in what often felt like an abandoned forest. Nearly every day was a scene straight out of a Brother's Grimm classic.

"Don't worry, it's gonna be fine," I comforted Tootie.

Driver's door open, I could barely see over the steering wheel. Half of my 80-pound frame hung tightly on the wheel while the other half was clinging to the dirt. My 11-year-old sister was at the rear, pushing for dear life. Small as we were, it's a miracle the car didn't take one of us out.

Halfway down the driveway, we had one eye on our front door, expecting Mom to come screaming out, switch in hand.

The early-morning silence was our green light. I slid behind the wheel, ready to get this driving party started.

Self-reliance had a sound: engine growls and grinding gears. As my confidence and fearlessness grew, I was determined to go farther every time.

But Mom's "hawk eye" was practically a sixth sense.

"Don't tell me a story, Neekie—I SAW you out there in my car!" she shouted one morning, voice ricocheting off the trailer's wood-paneled walls.

For me, every mission to the grocery store, every carefully stretched Food Stamp, and every awkward dodge of police and friends helped me imagine a future beyond Prattville (which my sister and I called Crapville).

Like Hansel and Gretel, I learned early that survival doesn't come from waiting to be saved (or waiting for the prince charming Mom kept confusing with the savior in the Bible).

Taking the wheel meant stepping out, facing fears, and finding the way—one breadcrumb at a time.

Her eyes flicked toward the switch hanging by the door. I froze, my backside tense in anticipation. But instead, something shifted. Mom's anger melted into what looked like acceptance—or maybe opportunity.

With a sigh, she threw me the keys. "Well then, you're goin' to the store. We need milk, and I need tampons."

*TAMPONS! Gross!*

Mom's decision to let a pre-teen drive to town and grocery shop was a contradiction. For a woman who ruled our lives through a mix of folklore, fairytales and the 10 Commandments, the lines between morality and survival were often a blur. Maybe it was necessity, trust born out of desperation.

*The Expert Generalist Lesson #14*
## TAKE THE WHEEL

When you jump into the driver's seat of any situation—even if you don't know exactly what you're doing—you open the door to possibility. Taking the lead doesn't mean having all the answers; it means you're willing to steer into the unknown and navigate challenges as they come.

So go on, take some calculated risks, even if it means 'borrowing' your mom's car.

# CHAPTER FIFTEEN

**IT WAS CLUTTERED AND CHAOTIC**—A PLACE WHERE LED ZEPPELIN BLARED, **& THE STENCH OF CIGARETTES LINGERED** AMONG OTHER THINGS THEY SMOKED.

# SALSA & SURVIVAL

The payphone hung on the wall near the kitchen; its receiver smudged from hunters just out of the Alaskan Bush. It rarely rang. When it did, it was bad news—or worse, someone looking for you.

"Monique! Phone for you!" Laurie's voice carried over the sizzle of fajitas and clatter of dishes at Gordos. I wiped my hands on my apron, stomach tightening.

"It's your dad," Laurie whispered, stepping back toward the kitchen.

The cord twisted in my fingers as I pressed the receiver to my ear.

"Hello?" I said, bracing. At 16, I had moved to Alaska after a long summer at odds with Mom.

My dad's voice came through, flat and mechanical. "Annie doesn't want you here anymore."

The words sounded like they came off a well-rehearsed script, Annie likely miming from backstage.

"What?" I said.

He didn't elaborate. "You'll have to figure something out."

Then silence. I swallowed the lump rising in my throat.

"Okay." I hung up and leaned against the wall.

Tears welled as the kitchen door swung open and Laurie returned, full of questions.

I didn't drink, smoke, date, or sneak out, but Annie couldn't stand having me there. A 26-year-old stepmother (wife #5) married to a 43-year-old father had decided my fate. Maybe it was jealousy. Maybe insecurity.

By the time my shift ended, I had already started making mental checklists. *Where could I stay tonight? How much would I have to save for a one-way ticket back to Alabama?*

Three months after touching down in Alaska, I was forced to couch surf in a town where I knew almost no one. I felt like one of Mom's stray dogs, thrown out like trash at the end of the road.

First up was my new friend Cyndie's house. She was the first person I met in Fairbanks and had quickly become my best friend.

Cyndie and her parents had already gotten an ominous call from Annie. They were Southerners, too, and good humans who fed me real meals like fried chicken and mashed potatoes, not the single boiled egg my dad used to send me to school with.

"You can stay here as long as you want."

Cyndie's parents saw more in me than my own family. They saw an intelligent, independent, hard-working young woman who had never known real support.

At work, I would fill up on chips and salsa every night. On the weekends, I worked doubles, serving and wiping tables until my arms ached. Sade crooned through the speakers, her voice softening the sharp edges of my exhaustion. Laurie's apartment came next. It was cluttered and chaotic—a place where Led Zeppelin blared, and the stench of cigarettes lingered among other things they smoked. We stayed up late, talking about nothing and everything. She made me laugh even when I wanted to scream.

Most nights, I collapsed on Laurie's couch, still in uniform, counting tips and tips alone—quarters, crumpled ones, an occasional five. Each dollar pushed me closer to what I needed for my exodus back home.

School became an afterthought, a box I checked while plotting my exit. Still, I was making straight A's. Somehow, school was always easier than my life.

On April Fool's Day, I boarded the plane with a single suitcase. The absurdity of the whole experience was so perfectly encapsulated by that date, I sometimes thought, *Was the joke on me?*

My seatbelt clicked and I exhaled for the first time in months. Alabama waited, humid and familiar. But this time, I would be in charge.

I had learned to survive completely on my own—how to make every dollar count, couch surf with grace, and still show up to fulfill my responsibilities at school and work.

Like a failed gold miner, it was the second time moving to Alaska had ended with a life-changing decision, made for me.

This time, I would never be fooled again. Or so I thought.

> # "THE ONLY PERSON YOU ARE DESTINED TO BECOME IS THE PERSON YOU DECIDE TO BE."
> ## -RALPH WALDO EMERSON

*The Expert Generalist Lesson #15*
## SAVE YOURSELF

You can choose to live in a mindset of "why is this happening to me?" Or...you can embrace the belief that life happens for you, not to you. Genuine self-reliance is about stepping up and finding solutions when life takes unexpected turns. Adapting, staying resourceful, and moving forward—no matter the circumstance—are choices only *you* can make.

# CHAPTER SIXTEEN

# THE GREAT EQUALIZER

Part of moving to Alaska was to get a tuition waiver for college. My dad was a professor and the schtick was that I would've gotten a four-year university degree, 100 percent gratis.

Growing up, I didn't have much hope of going to college. It just didn't seem like an option for someone like me. Few from my family graduated high school, let alone earned a bachelor's. But when I got back from Alaska, all my YMCA friends seemed to talk about was Auburn University.

Once upon a time, my dream had been to be a trailer park kid. My sister and I would long to trade our isolated hilltop for the chance to be part of a community.

In a way, I manifested this reality, but with college students and keggers. I made it to Auburn, where all the cool kids lived in a trailer park.

Without any financial help from my family, I had no choice but to do what I always did to make it work: work.

I was soon back to my roots as a hustler—usually juggling three to four jobs at a time: I waited tables (at a place aptly called the Plantation), lifeguarded and managed at three pools, babysat, tutored, sold clothing at Gayfer's department store, started a kids program at the Country Club, decorated Christmas trees for hire, attended the window at the dry cleaning drive-thru, and more.

At Auburn, I delivered equipment to classrooms and worked at the Alumni Center doing what we called "dialing for dollars." I even wrote papers for frat boys. $50 a pop was good money in those days.

Working was my runner's high. It still is. Landing a contract, training a room full of executives, traveling across the world to host a retreat—it's all an adrenaline rush.

Hard as I worked, I still knew the power (and importance) of play. Three days into my first quarter, I found myself at a band party at the SAE house. We dragged beer in gallon jugs from Momma G's, a package store on frat row that never checked IDs.

This was not just my first real party and live concert, but it was also the biggest stage I had ever seen. Soon after the party got started, I saw him. Charlie Daniels.

I froze. *No way.*

I pushed through the crowd until I was standing close enough to see the subtle sway of his beard and ten gallon cowboy hat. He ripped

into his fiddle, and the crowd exploded as if we'd been waiting for this moment our whole lives. I stood in the middle of it all, thinking, *Is this my life now?*

Auburn was the start of my global network. Fraternity band parties meant brushing shoulders with international athletes and politicians' kids (that's how I ended up staying overnight at Senator Callahan's house, but that's another story).

I wasn't the kind of person who would go to a band party and only talk to people I knew. Friends would playfully joke that I could talk to a wall. I could strike up a conversation with anyone, and often did!

Thanks to my sincere curiosity about people's stories and my gregarious nature, my circle of influence ballooned alongside my Rolodex. Before long, I had three sheets of typed paper full of 125 names that I would often call one by one.

"Hey, is there a party tonight?"
"Hey, is there a party tonight?"
"Hey, is there a party tonight?"

Pretty soon, I was the first call on everyone's list.

Magical things were happening around me. My belief is that going to college was and still is a great equalizer. People don't see where or how you grew up. You're either in a dorm, an apartment, or (in Auburn) a trailer.

Nobody knew my financial status. Whether I was at the senator's house, a band party, or a football game, I fit right in. All it took was the unofficial 1990s college uniform: band party tee, Duck Head shorts (I had a pair in every color), hair bow, and ASICS.

Sure, sometimes my cover was blown when someone's face lit up with recognition. "Are you the drive-thru dry cleaner girl?"

I used to feel like everyone in my life had a headstart other than me. College was my chance to catch up...and soon enough, pull ahead.

I was out almost every night—Greek parties, live music, and bonfires stretched until dawn. But no matter how late I stayed out, I was at the pool by 5:30am, turning the key to open up for morning lap swim.

The rhythm of my life pulsed like a song—work, class, work, party, repeat.

Growing up, dancing was free. And by 1991, dancing was my freedom.

That was when U2's *Achtung Baby* dropped and I was obsessed. I had not yet felt 'love' in the sense of the word. But I fell in love with U2 that year and still feel just as deeply today.

When their tour came through Birmingham, I scraped together just enough for a ticket. The crowd was a blur as I bolted to the third row. Knowing my seat was in the nosebleeds, I begged the other fans (who'd paid quite a lot more than I did) to let me stand next to them. My face beamed with glee when they obliged.

I knew every word to every song and sang until my voice was hoarse, fully lost in the music. Somewhere between the lights and the lyrics, something shifted. It hit me that this wasn't just about music, parties, or escape.

This moment in my life was about breaking free: everything I had known—including my mother's abusive reign—was over. No one could tell me "no"...that girls like me didn't go to college, didn't travel, didn't dream too big.

From here on out, life was mine to chart. I was more than equal.

## *The Expert Generalist Lesson #16*
# YOU CAN DO IT ALL

Success and happiness, work and play—it's all possible. You can carve out space for ambition, while chasing joy and managing responsibilities. The key lies in how you organize, set boundaries, and allocate your energy. When you approach life with the belief that it *is* possible to do it all, you'll find that you have much more bandwidth than you think.

# CHAPTER SEVENTEEN

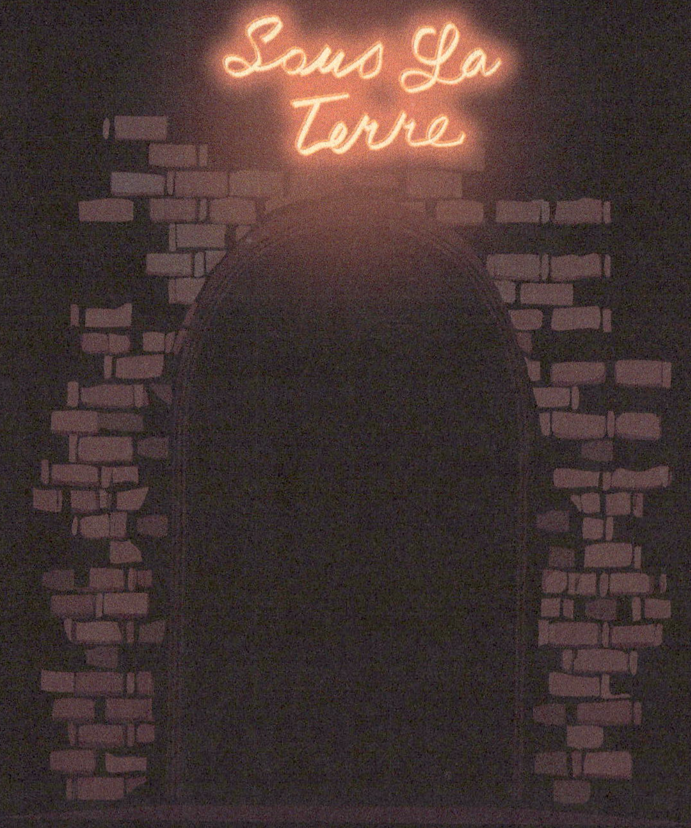

# FISH OUT OF WATER

The bouncer didn't even blink as we handed over our crumpled bills.

"Cash talks, bullshit walks," someone muttered.

That's how we found ourselves in what felt like a scene straight out of *Adventures in Babysitting*.

To this day, the spontaneous road trip remains one of my favorite college escapades.

"It's only an hour away and we can stay at my Mom's house; she's out of town," my friend and fellow lifeguard described a scene too alluring to pass up. My zest for questionable adventure had stuck with me since the go-kart days.

In a blink, we piled into a friend's SUV and headed to the underground jazz and blues bar.

Every night felt like another audacious dare. *Could I even get in? Who would I meet?*

Sous La Terre was a legendary spot for live music in Montgomery, complete with a red carpet staircase winding down to a smoky, dim-lit room.

As we stepped inside, the whole bar seemed to turn and stare. It wasn't just the fact that we were white kids in a place we had no business being, but we looked like we'd wandered in from a middle school field trip.

"Y'all new here, right?" the bartender said, after extending his palm for more cash. Before I could respond, I felt a hand on my shoulder. Suddenly, I was being ushered to the stage.

"Sit here," the lead singer grinned, propping me onto a stool in the spotlight. The crowd stared in silence until the band strung the first chord to "Hoochie Coochie Man" by Muddy Waters. I froze for a second, then leaned in, laughing at how surreal it felt to be on stage three hours after we made the decision to leave Auburn.

"Hand me my drink," I said, smiling from my new perch. It doesn't get any more front row than that!

The song echoed through the smoky bar, and I couldn't help but feel I was right where I was supposed to be. It wasn't about drinking or rebellion; it was about pulling off another impossible feat and soaking up the music and energy in the room.

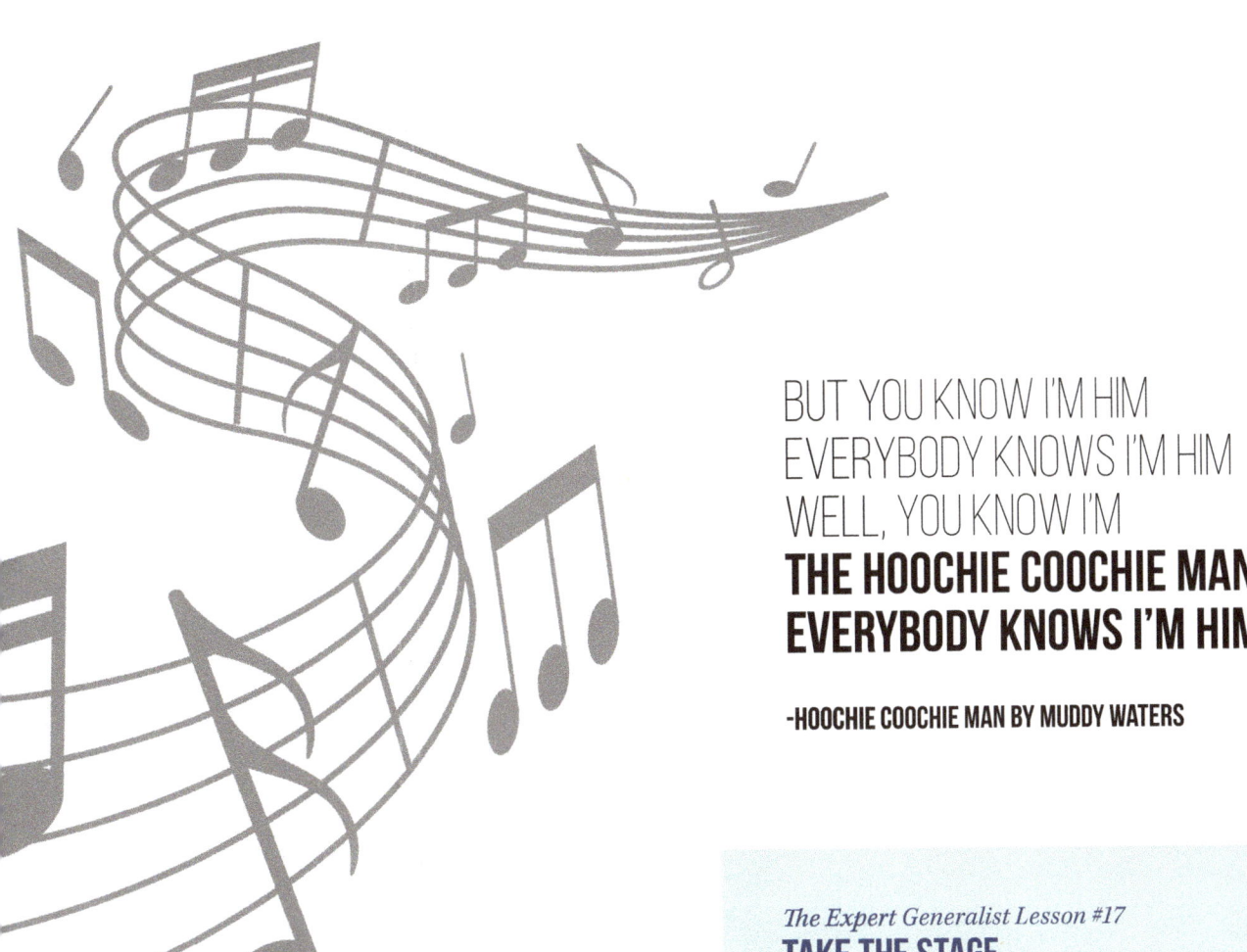

BUT YOU KNOW I'M HIM
EVERYBODY KNOWS I'M HIM
WELL, YOU KNOW I'M
**THE HOOCHIE COOCHIE MAN**
**EVERYBODY KNOWS I'M HIM**

**-HOOCHIE COOCHIE MAN BY MUDDY WATERS**

*The Expert Generalist Lesson #17*
### TAKE THE STAGE

Sometimes, you belong exactly where you don't. The idea of "fake it til you make it" isn't about pretending—it's about having the courage to show up and figure things out as you go. Whether stepping into a smoky bar or boardroom, success doesn't come from being perfect; it comes from leaning in and seizing the moment.

Life rewards those who take the stage.

# CHAPTER EIGHTEEN

# CONTAGION

He stood on a catawampus wooden crate, the makeshift pulpit wobbling under the weight of his wrath. I thought I'd left these jokers behind in Prattville.

But there he was: Brother Jed, the self-proclaimed street preacher—transforming campuses in the South into a stage for venomous sermons. He was the opposite of the Jesus I had grown up learning about.

One afternoon, as my friends and I walked back from the pool in our cut-off Daisy Dukes, his baseless judgements hurled through the air.

"You whore! You slut!" he branded us to everyone in earshot, having found his mark for the day.

Auburn's Concourse, usually alive with energy and movement, suddenly felt suffocating. Many students drowned him out with music from their Discmans, but his presence was equally as unavoidable as it was disturbing.

"Who are you to judge me?" I raged back, indignant and fueled by MY Southern Christian upbringing. "You don't know my life. You're just making up stories because you don't like my shorts."

Brother Jed's intention to "save souls" had the opposite effect—it drove me further from the biblical teachings that had been forced on me as a child. His presence reminded me of the traveling preachers and their mobile revivals. Total fraudsters armed with nothing but scare tactics (and sometimes, live snakes).

The hypocrisy of Brother Jed was the nail in the coffin of my evangelical leaning. His words didn't reflect the love and grace I'd been taught to associate with faith. Instead, they embodied ignorance, hatred, and toxicity.

During those transformative years, I had begun to question the validity of it all and often wondered, *Is there even a God?*

# "YOU WHORE! YOU SLUT!"

HE BRANDED US TO EVERYONE IN EARSHOT, HAVING FOUND HIS MARK FOR THE DAY.

*The Expert Generalist Lesson #18*
## YOU ARE WHAT YOU EAT

Hatred and ignorance are contagious. The good news is: love and kindness are, too! We are shaped by what we allow into our lives—whether it's the media we consume, the food we eat, our daily habits, or the people we surround ourselves with. Choose wisely.

# CHAPTER NINETEEN

MY LIFE AS A COASTAL
COWGIRL **HAD ALREADY
BEGUN TO MANIFEST.**

# ROAD MAPS & REVELATIONS

My vision for when I graduated college was far bigger than an M.R.S. degree or settling down in Birmingham or Atlanta. My sights were set on something completely different: pioneering a new life in the Great American West.

This seed was planted during a road trip that changed everything. It all started with Chris, a guy I met at a band party.

He was different—no accent, no twang—straight out of Miami and worlds apart from the small-town Alabama crowd I was used to. Even more than that, Chris had something I didn't: a Ford Explorer. The name itself was perfectly fitting already.

Chris turned out to be my ultimate partner in crime, up for anything. Soon enough, we hatched a plan to hit the open road. Armed with an atlas and an AAA TripTik, we camped in Arkansas, toured the University of Colorado, and marveled at Rocky Mountain National Park.

Apart from flying over mountains, I had never experienced them up close, even in Alaska. Turns out, I was a Mountain Girl at heart all along and never knew it.

The journey took us all the way to Medford, Oregon—where I would couch surf for a second time with my friend Laurie (who'd moved there from Alaska).

I couldn't stop talking about how I wanted to bring back a legit, Stetson cowboy hat as a souvenir. One afternoon, Chris and I were lost in the Siskiyou Mountains. We ended up turning onto an unpaved road. I kid you not, a brown felt Stetson was sitting there in the dirt.

Chris and I had to do a double take. We couldn't believe our eyes.

"Should I keep it?" I chuckled.

My life as a coastal cowgirl had already begun to manifest.

From there, we drove into San Francisco. I'll never forget the moment we crossed the Golden Gate Bridge, with Ziggy Marley playing a live set for the local radio. I'd never seen a big city like that, skyscrapers mixed with rolling hills and fog. It was equal parts overwhelming and awe-inspiring.

We wandered the waterfront, explored Chinatown, and even walked into the iconic Fairmont Hotel on Nob Hill. I never could have imagined that, years later, this would be my

backyard while I worked with Fortune 100 companies—or that someone would throw my surprise 40th birthday party at that very same Fairmont. *Tonga Room and Mai Tais anyone?!*

San Francisco felt like being in a movie. I remember vividly turning the wrong way down a one-way and almost bumping into a streetcar. Horns blared as we scrambled to figure out where we were.

Pre-internet, pre-smartphone—being lost was part of the adventure.

# I KID YOU NOT, A BROWN FELT STETSON WAS SITTING THERE IN THE DIRT.

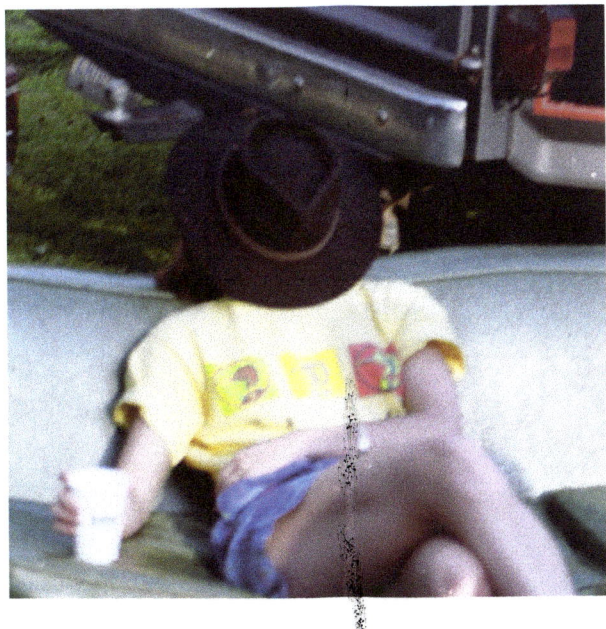

On the drive back to Auburn, I couldn't stop thinking about how to make my way back to build a life there. The trip was the first time I felt the pull of the West. Thanks to the crisp San Francisco breeze, wide-open spaces, and grandeur of the Rockies, I could finally put a feeling to the future I'd pictured for myself.

Going west in the land of opportunity meant proving that I was more than Alabama, much more.

*The Expert Generalist Lesson #19*
## SAY YES...

To more

***Adventure, Challenges, Invitations, Awkwardness, Conversations.***

Life is like a road trip—with the whispers of the wind inviting you to explore new places, take detours, and meet people who are different from you. Saying YES will put you on the map for a journey filled with growth, meaning, and unforgettable memories.

# CHAPTER TWENTY

# THE AUBURN
## CREED

I BELIEVE THAT THIS IS A PRACTICAL
WORLD AND THAT I CAN COUNT
ONLY ON WHAT I EARN. THEREFORE,
I BELIEVE IN WORK, HARD WORK...

---

AND BECAUSE AUBURN MEN AND
WOMEN BELIEVE IN THESE THINGS,

## I BELIEVE IN
## AUBURN & LOVE IT.

-GEORGE PETRIE (1943)

# TOOT YOUR OWN HORN

"We are sorry to inform you..."

I stopped reading. A pit began to form in my stomach. The rejection stung even more since, up until then, I had gotten every job or role I had tried out or applied for.

After hours spent perfecting my application for the scholarship—detailing every campus club, job, and extracurricular—my friends were more sure than I was: no one at Auburn was a better fit.

My next step after college was all but decided. My plan was to move to Seattle to pursue a career in Interior Design. After growing up surrounded by deterioration, I was set on making things better.

This scholarship was literally the only way I could get there.

I stared at the rejection letter until the words blurred.

Soon, I heard through the rumor mill that the person who got the money didn't even have a job (which was a specific requirement on the application).

*Um, what?*

Despite having worked more jobs than anyone I knew, I was still struggling. School was $395 a quarter and the Pell Grant grant covered it in full thanks to my family's income (or lack thereof). Even so, I would max out the loans on other expenses and still be pinching pennies. Once the disappointment, panic, and anger had passed, I went into Fix-It Mode.

The following day, I was in the Assistant Dean's office. On the edge of my chair, arms folded, I asked the only question I could think of.

"Why not me?"

Dr. Cavender looked up, putting a face to my name for the first time (When I graduated, she would be the only teacher who gave me a gift—a book I still have today.).

"You've done the work," she simply said. "Now make sure people know who you are."

That's when it hit me. Hard work isn't always loud enough. Sometimes, you need to announce it.

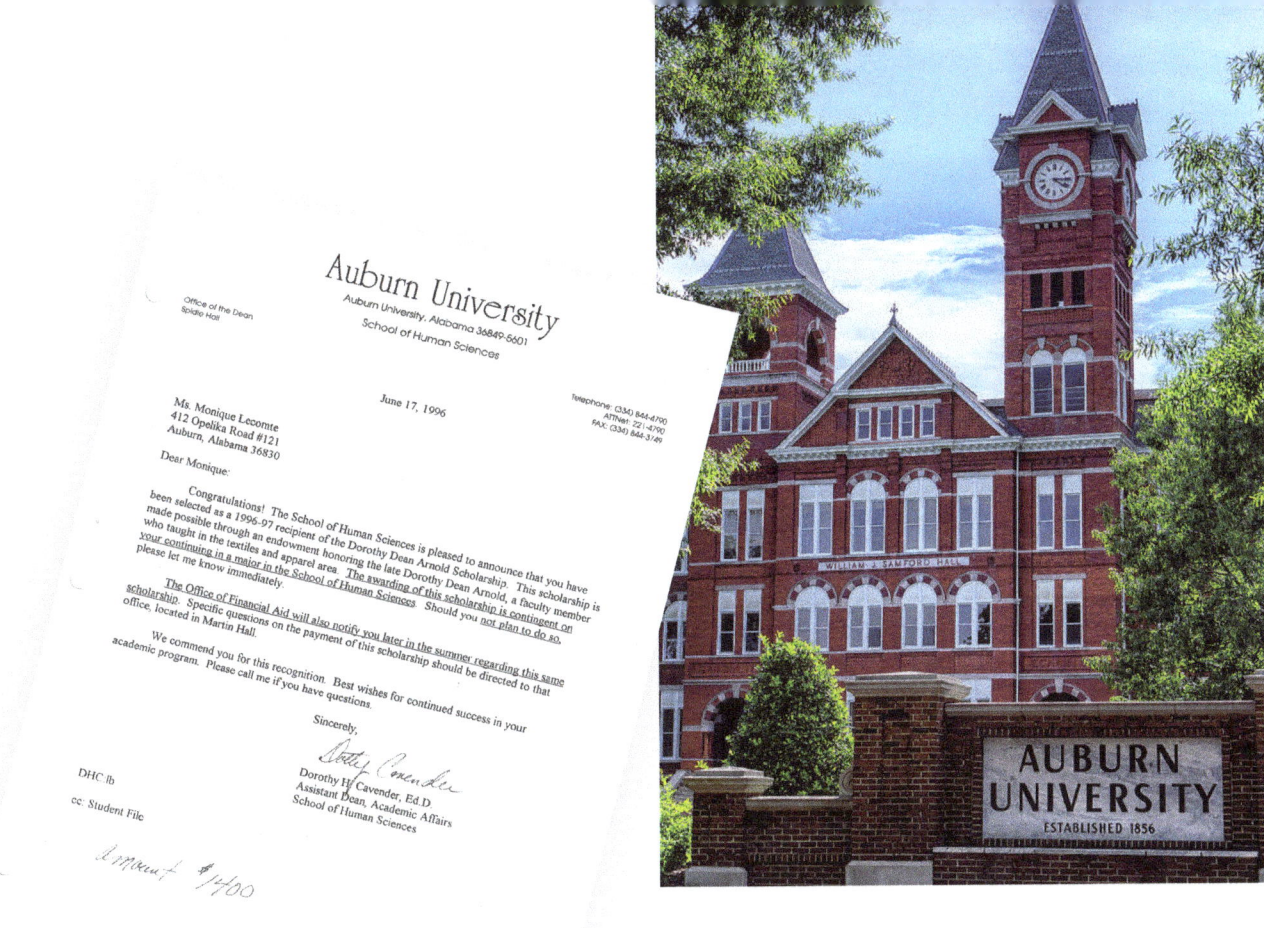

Even at age 20, I was the biggest Expert Generalist on campus. From then on out, it was up to me to let people know it.

A similar envelope arrived the next year. This time, the letter started with "Congratulations..."

Boy, I loved Auburn. I still do today! The Auburn Creed sums it up perfectly.

## ADVOCATE FOR YOURSELF

If you don't succeed at first, you'd better dig deeper, try harder, or get more creative at making your case. In this world, you've got to toot your own horn—loud and proud—and clearly ask for what you want. No one's going to read your mind.

If you don't speak up for yourself, who will?

# CHAPTER TWENTY ONE

EVERYBODY ELSE IS MOVING THERE,
**SHOULD YOU?**

# RAIN CHECK

Have you ever experienced those moments in life when everything seems to align perfectly, almost as if the universe is giving you a nudge? Some call it being in the flow—like catching every green light on your path.

And then, you walk into the Winn Dixie and see a rack full of Newsweeks. A Seattle man on the cover in a yellow slicker holds a Salmon and proclaims: *Everybody Else is Moving There, Should You?*

I trusted signs. I knew what this meant. After two years of dreaming about it, my move West was officially in the stars.

Clocking in at 2.7 million people in the 1990s, Seattle was *90 times* bigger than the 30,000ish population of each Auburn and Fairbanks. This was my chance to 'make it in the big city.' My own Manifest Destiny felt near predestined.

One afternoon, I stood up at a Tiger Splashers meeting (the social arm for Auburn's Swimming & Diving team).

"Hey everybody, I'm moving to Seattle. If anyone wants to join, come see me after the meeting!"

A gal named Kyle stepped right up. "I'm in."

She graduated first and ended up driving all the way back from Michigan to pick me up. We piled everything I owned (pretty much just clothes and my drawing & drafting materials) into her grey Honda Civic. And off we went.

In Seattle, I soon discovered that my small-town values and way of life weren't just a hindrance...they seemed to make me the butt of every joke.

"What did you just say?" People either truly couldn't understand my accent or wanted to make a point that my Southern dictionary wasn't going to translate. And NObody was interested in talking about SEC football.

This is the one time in my life that being young didn't work to my benefit.

*I wish I was 30, so people would take me seriously*, I used to think.

During the two years I'd worked my tail off to save up, I had the vision that my new life would be just like the movies: making new friends left and right, nightly happy hours, ferry rides to nearby islands—all with the backdrop of the Space Needle.

Not so much.

You know that little statue, with arms open wide that says, "I love you this much"? Before long, I came to experience a new Heisman Trophy approach, with a stiff arm and flat palm silently indicating, "Hello, you can stay this length from me, thank you."

Some people call it the "Seattle Freeze": a laid-back, yet distant vibe where people are friendly but keep their emotions and connections at arm's length.

There were no invites to BBQs, let alone casseroles passed around when new families moved in. Borrowing eggs or sugar was a hard no. And the flake-factor was undeniable. I've lost track of how many seats I would excitedly save, only to end up eating out alone, or just me and Kyle.

This was my first time not knowing my neighbors and I still find it bizarre that people live in such an isolated way. It's no wonder we are in a loneliness epidemic.

The hot, humid skies I'd known were replaced by nine months of gray, near-constant drizzle. Oh, and I was riding the bus again. My design internship was 1.5 hours each way, including a transfer downtown. I had traded a bunch of rowdy schoolkids for a series of wild, public bus characters from what was considered the "Heroin Capital" of the U.S. at the time.

*Was this a sign of things to come?*

My next rude awakening was the cost. Rent in Auburn was $95 a month, thanks to a scrappy, creative living situation that was our version of *Melrose Place* (concocted by yours truly, of course). It was cheap, chaotic, close-quarters, and we loved it.

Seattle was a whole different show. Splitting my first apartment cost five times as much, and that didn't include the utilities or groceries that doubled in price just for being surrounded by skyscrapers.

When I landed my first role as an Interior Designer with Sechrist Design Associates, I thought I'd made it. I was making $19,000 a year, which was more than my mom had ever and would ever make.

Turns out, in Seattle, that wage was near poverty level. I had gone from being poor in the woods to living in an apartment where a rat literally ate through our dishwasher.

I soon picked up several other hustles to make ends meet, returning to my roots as a waitress, gopher girl, and nanny—often clocking 70-80 hours each week. If my Alabama upbringing had taught me anything, it was the value of hard work.

To match my fancy new lifestyle, I leased a brand new car. In college, I would cruise to my various jobs in a white 1963 Plymouth Valiant, until it died. Next, I had a baby blue 1973 Cadillac Deville (which I often got pulled over

in, the cops thinking someone very different was driving).

Modest by city standards, my shiny black Honda Accord symbolized progress. At the time, I didn't realize how much pressure that "progress" would put on my finances.

Seattle wasn't just a place—it was trial by error. My decade there would test my adaptability to a totally foreign way of life, my persona as a businesswoman, and my ability to grow a highfalutin new network from scratch.

Despite the rocky start, I have lifelong friends and confidants in The Emerald City to this day.

Though challenging and fully different from my expectations, I wouldn't trade those early struggles for anything. They built the foundation for how I have been able to navigate everything that has come since.

*The Expert Generalist Lesson #21*
## ENERGY ATTRACTS ENERGY

Put yourself out there and see what sticks. If you don't say it or think it, how is it going to show up in your life? The simple act of putting your vision into words and actions will create a ripple effect beyond your wildest dreams. Whether it's a new project, an idea, or a request for help, share it. You might just be amazed at what comes back like a boomerang.

# CHAPTER TWENTY TWO

# ALONE

**D**ing, Ding." The flight was boarding my connection to Costa Rica. I was getting married.

In 2000, destination weddings weren't the thing they are now, so getting 40 of my closest friends together with my family to fly abroad was a big deal. Most of them didn't even have passports!

"You could have been in better shape," my soon-to-be husband whispered the sweet nothing into my ear.

And there it was—that sick, sinking feeling that I often had throughout my three years with this guy.

If you've been with me this far, you might be wondering how a strong, independent, badass woman could end up in the crosshairs of a guy like this.

And that's just it. Sometimes those very type Alpha, highly successful people are specifically targeted by abusers. Although narcissism is often confused with self-absorption, the true clinical "narcissist" could win a medal in:

## GASLIGHTING

*gas·lie·ting*

*verb*

refers to a form of psychological manipulation where someone causes another person to doubt their perceptions, memories, or sanity over time. This technique is often used to gain control or maintain power in a relationship.

Before then, I had never heard of those terms—a true testament to life prior to the Digital Era, or even, a cell phone.

It doesn't matter if they show up with flowers, gnaw your ear off for hours that it'll never happen again, or do some borderline-stalker behavior that feels over-the-top but somehow loving...the dark side will always, and I do mean always, return to take control.

My mom's "Suck it up" mantra had unsurprisingly backfired by turning me into too tough of a girl. Not allowed to date growing up, I had no clue how to navigate this level of affection, attention, attraction, or abuse. "Nobody's ever going to love you as much as I do," he'd say, after covering my screaming mouth while holding me down on the ground until my wrists were bruised.

This must be love. No one had ever said those magic three words or touched me in the good and bad ways that he had. And, according to Brother Jed, now that I was officially a "woman," the decision had been made for me.

Sitting on that plane, I felt trapped, careening toward a future I knew in my heart would be a life sentence.

Christmases, holidays, and birthdays were full of a grotesque amount of love bombs and gift giving, all with a web of strings attached. This contrasted with moments like when my laptop was kicked down the stairs in a fit of rage. His constant belittling of me knew no bounds. If I said red, he said green. Every day was a mind fuck and I had somehow been brainwashed to believe it was all me.

Back then, I was too inexperienced and innocent to realize that people's words don't always match up with their actions. And, more importantly, when that's the case: RUN. Run like your life depends on it, because sometimes ... it does.

I would drag a 280 lb anchor around for 17 years.

*The Expert Generalist Lesson #22*
## CHOOSE WISELY

Narcissists are like magicians—masters of illusion. It's not love; it's the ultimate catfish. Learn to spot the signs (love-bombing, gaslighting, isolation, excessive control) and get out the moment you do.

LISTEN to your gut, protect your light, and remember—it's okay to kiss a few frogs along the way. Just don't marry them.

# CHAPTER TWENTY THREE

I BOUGHT A
CROSSCOUNTRY
PLANE TICKET
**WITHOUT TELLING
HIM OR ANYONE ELSE.**

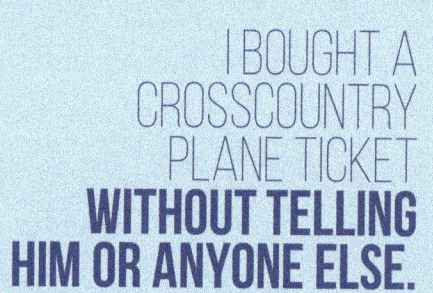

# FAMILY FIRST

When I was 26, I became the guardian of my little brother.

My mother had gotten pregnant in circumstances we don't talk about. At the same time, we're all grateful Christopher was born into our lives.

"Our electricity and water got turned off," he told me one day, by phone.

The moment we hung up, I bought a cross-country plane ticket without telling him or anyone else. That was the only way to get a realistic lay of the land.

Indeed, everything was turned off and their water bill was $1700. On top of the bare cupboards, there was garbage strewn across the yard, sewage flowing into a large hole down the hill, a leaking roof, floorboards so rotten you could see the ground, and stacks of unopened mail in hoarder piles—all amidst a potpourri of secondhand smoke and damp mold.

Gone was the sweet smell of Grandma's roses, mowed down by my mom's abusive alcoholic husband. He'd even cut down the only shade protecting them from the oppressive summer heat, selling our Loblolly Pines to the papermill for beer.

They'd spend any other money my mom had on gas to get water from artesian wells downtown and buy kerosene for the heater. Scary enough, that's often how people with no financial literacy do it: they plug the holes, in a way that ends up costing more than fixing the boat.

My mom's husband had taken over managing her trailer and her every movement—which

would drag on for a grand total of 30 years. Whenever I approached her about the chaos, she would stare blankly down or straight ahead blankly, like a scolded child.

I knew something serious was wrong but had no idea at the time that it could be early-onset Alzheimer's. We quickly buzzed around to doctors and a counselor to find treatment for what I thought was severe depression. Even though I feared for her life, she gave the performance of the century at all the appointments, as if nothing was wrong.

On that same trip, I learned that Christopher was about to fail the fifth grade. And it wasn't because he wasn't bright; no one was steering the ship at home.

He was alone, in a way that we never had been growing up. Everything was toxic. The air they breathed. The words they used. The drunken violence.

I made the decision to pay my mom's phone bills, so I would always have a connection to my little brother and he could call 911 if things went sideways. Thankfully, it was 1999 so I could demand to be his guardian without any paperwork. I flew down from Seattle to meet with his teachers every few months.

Things only got worse on each visit.

"If we don't intervene, he'll be taken by the state and we'll never see him again," I told my sister, Melissa (aka Tootie), the summer after Christopher's sixth grade.

She knew. She'd already stayed behind to watch over him for two years instead of going to college right away.

Melissa soon took Christopher and then he flew to Seattle until we could come up with a plan. Well, the plan never came.

"Don't make me go back," his red face was streaked with tears at the airport. I was balling too. I continued to cry until my new husband finally relented. Back I flew to Alabama to pick Christopher up.

That's when my husband stopped working. I think it was to punish me. From then on, all my finances went to support our life and somehow, to my husband's family but not mine. This would continue for 13 years.

In Seattle, Christopher encountered the same culture shock that I had, and then some. He went from a mobile home in the backwoods of Deatsville to going to school surrounded by Microsoft kids.

I was working 50-60 hours a week while tutoring my brother at night. We're not talking just the regular seventh grade curriculum, but all the tech that these advanced kids had grown up with.

"What's a PowerPoint?" School had changed by a country mile.

Fast forward to just before his high school graduation and my husband kicked Christopher out.

# EVEN THE MOST BROKEN PATHS CAN LEAD TO EXTRAORDINARY DESTINATIONS.

He spent a total of six years with me, going on business trips and experiencing my life. I introduced him to friends (some of whom were firefighters) and arranged for him to shadow a cadet at the Air Force Academy.

Now, Christopher is a firefighter in the Air Force, a husband to an EMT, and has seen more of the world than anyone in my family, including me!

Watching Christopher become the man he was meant to be—a protector, a provider, and a source of strength—proves that even the most broken paths can lead to extraordinary destinations.

*The Expert Generalist Lesson #23*
## STEP UP

Life doesn't wait for you to feel ready—it just shows up and makes demands. What matters is being fully present and giving something your all, especially if it means helping someone in need.

When the moment calls for it, *step up*.

# CHAPTER TWENTY FOUR

We are all

Leaders

-Peter Drucker

# SERVANT LEADERSHIP

I still remember sitting in the conference room for my first 360° review at Herman Miller, the iconic furniture company known for the Aeron chair.

I had moved the three of us to Denver for this job and I was the only breadwinner.

*What if the feedback was something I couldn't fix? What if it was personal?*

My manager (who happened to be one of the nicest men I've ever met) began to speak and the tension in my chest immediately loosened.

This wasn't a teardown or a list of failures. It was a thoughtful, balanced conversation. For every critique, there was encouragement and actionable insight. It felt different—like I wasn't just in a job, but building a career.

Then came the line that hit hardest. It had been written by my sales partner, Mike Doody, who had seen me in work mode more than anyone else.

"Monique is a strong leader, but she sometimes hesitates to ask for help."

At first, it stung. I prided myself on being fiercely independent—hearing that felt like a judgment. But, I knew the intention behind Doody's words because I knew Doody.

"This isn't about weakness," my manager explained. "It's about giving others the opportunity to support you, just as you support them."

Herman Miller's founder, D.J. De Pree, led by the decree of Servant Leadership. He believed in treating everyone from the janitor to the C-suite with the same level of respect.

This style of leadership wasn't just lip service—it was lived out every day. Through a culture of trust, innovation, and collaboration, Herman Miller became a model of ethical and progressive leadership.

Come to think of it, my most significant periods of growth in life ALL came directly from feedback. Constructive input, even the kind you don't want to hear, helps you grow. Period.

This shift in perspective is transformational.

**EACH STAR LED HER TO THE NEXT UNTIL... SHE HAD SUCCEEDED IN WEAVING TOGETHER A LIFE FILLED WITH ALL THE GOOD THINGS SHE COULD IMAGINE.**

Later in my career, I spent two cringe-worthy years working for the polar opposite kind of "leader." Every conversation was a field of landmines. The culture was toxic and meetings were a two-faced performance disguised as collaboration. Feedback without trust felt like a weapon and passive-aggressive comments destroyed our teams.

Experiencing the full spectrum of leadership, or lack thereof, inspired me to start my own company. Now, I proudly train professionals into unstoppable leaders with the skills to embrace adversity, welcome challenges, and build safe spaces.

# SERVANT LEADERSHIP

*sur-vuhnt*
*leed-er-ship*
*noun*
a philosophy that prioritizes the needs of others. It is a people-centered approach focused on collaboration, empathy, and ethical practices rather than authority and command. The leader's primary role is to serve their team, organization, and community.

## BE FEEDBACK-FUELED

Growth requires an open mind and a willingness to objectively listen to the perspectives of others. To sharpen your skills and understand how you truly show up, it's essential to separate fact from fiction. One of the most powerful tools for this practice is embracing constructive input from *trusted* sources.

By seeking and valuing their insight, you create a pathway for continuous improvement and self-awareness.

# CHAPTER TWENTY FIVE

AFTER WATCHING PETER PAN WHEN
I WAS FOUR, I WOULD OFTEN JUMP
OFF THE PORCH STEPS SHOUTING,

# THREE

# TWO

# ONE

FOR A SPLIT SECOND, IT FELT
LIKE I WAS FLYING.

# THREE, TWO, ONE

I t's just me and you tonight."

My eyes widened. *Is this it? Did my luck finally run out?*

I had ended up in Kiruna, a dot of a town on the northern tip of Sweden. Travel had become both my medicine and my escape. By then, I was on the road 250+ days a year.

That trip took me to the Stockholm Furniture Fair and I figured, why not take the opportunity to chase the Northern Lights? I had read about the smallest restaurant in the world and immediately booked my stay at the Arctic Gourmet Cabin. As I always did, I'd figure the rest out later.

"How are you going to get here?" the husband, who was part owner, asked via email.

"I'll grab an Uber."

"Think again," he'd essentially written back. Turns out, ride sharing hadn't made it 150 miles above the Arctic Circle.

He picked me up from the tiny airport and that's when he told me that the wife and kids were gone for the night.

I sat there in the front seat, stunned into silence. It felt like a moment straight out of a horror film.

Instead, Kiruna was just as magical as any of my other trips. I went dogsledding in the Narnia-esq landscape that was 23 degrees below, I drank Swedish beer in the original Icehotel, my hair froze in the hot tub, and I had a two-table restaurant—all to myself.

Snow on the ground, almost all 10 courses of my exceptional meal were cooked over an open fire. As I savored the darkness, I felt that familiar spark—the same one that had pushed me to leap into the unknown my whole life.

After watching *Peter Pan* when I was four, I would often jump off the porch steps shouting, "Three, two, one!" For a split second, it felt like I was flying. It's long been in my DNA to live life as an adventure.

Travel is often like looking through a kaleidoscope—suddenly, everything shifts, and you see the world in vibrant, unexpected patterns you won't find in the monotony of your daily grind. Without distractions or obligations, thoughts expand, and unexpected connections start to form.

For me, solo travel has always been where the best ideas take root. There's something about sitting on a quiet beach in Mallorca, hiking an empty trail in the Pyrenees, or walking through a bustling market in Mexico City that frees the mind.

So, where are you going to go? Two stars to the left is all you need to know.

*Lycklig resa!*

Every solo trip I've taken has been a catalyst for something bigger. It's where I've dreamed up new projects, solved seemingly impossible problems, and reconnected with myself. The world has so much to offer, but the real treasure is the perspective you gain and the ideas you bring back.

*The Expert Generalist Lesson #25*
## EMBRACE SOLITUDE

Solitude isn't something to fear—it's an invitation to just be. In the quiet, your mind finds room to dream, solve, and create. Step away from the noise, unplug, and take a moment (or a month-long trip) to rediscover yourself. You'll be amazed at what's waiting for you in the stillness.

# CHAPTER TWENTY SIX

# BE CAREFUL
## *THE COMPANY YOU KEEP*

# BLACK SWAN

Growing up in Alabama, I learned early to keep my eyes on the ground. Water moccasins were everywhere—quiet, hidden, and deadly if ignored. But living in big cities taught me that the most dangerous 'snakes' aren't the ones slithering. They are the people with power and privilege, made slick with their tech-adjacent prosperity.

One in particular was described to me as *"the town sleazeball."* Still, he initially seemed different—well-dressed, charming, and almost good-looking.

*Could people be that scandalous in real life?* I wondered. Maybe the rumor mill had gotten a little overzealous.

When I told my mentor I was meeting this person, she gave me a warning I'll never forget, "Don't you EVER get on one of those planes with them!"

That hit hard. She knew something I hadn't figured out yet. There are people who live in a world where integrity isn't just ignored; it is actively sacrificed. They set the table with champagne, cocaine, and compromise—flying their wedding-ring tan lines into Vegas like it was an Olympic sport.

The event? Catch & Release … of women, and countless of them.

These new-money bros normalize bad behavior to a level I have never seen before.

If someone is lying to their family, don't you think they're going to be deceitful to you? That person is the same person.

I see now that these are the signs of a covert narcissist hunting their prey for the next Black Swan Event.

## BLACK SWAN EVENT

*blak*
*swon*
*ee-vent*

*noun*
an unexpected and, therefore, difficult to prepare for life experience that changes everything; it is often rationalized as having been unavoidable in hindsight.

The saddest part is that these types of 'leaders' have destroyed countless lives. I know too many people who have lost their families, ended up in rehab, had to leave town, or worse.

Thankfully, the good outnumber the bad and I truly believe that. For every morally bankrupt person I've encountered, there are so many more who are salt of the earth—the kind of people who inspire you to be better simply by how they show up in the world, with no money or strings attached.

The genuine connections I've built over the years remind me what really matters: living in integrity and surrounding myself with people who do the same.

"What will grow crooked, you can't make straight
It's the price that you gotta pay

Do yourself a favor and pack your bags

Buy a ticket and get on the train
Buy a ticket and get on the train

Cause this is fucked up, fucked up
Cause this is fucked up, fucked up"

*-Black Swan by Thom Yorke*

*The Expert Generalist Lesson #26*
## WATCH THE WALK, IGNORE THE TALK

Planes or trains—take your pick. But never board the Hot
Mess Express, especially with those who don't walk their
talk. Surround yourself with people whose actions match
their words. Choose integrity over flash, and you'll never
have to question the destination.

# CHAPTER TWENTY SEVEN

# Barb was Magic

# WWBD?

**B**arb Carlyle didn't keep score. In all things business and personal, Barb was there to teach and never judge.

On the golf course, if everyone was playing poorly enough by the third hole, she would literally rip up our scorecards.

"We're playing for fun today!" she'd say, wearing her classic leopard-print long-sleeve and massive visor.

Barb had three biological kids but the number of people who consider her a mother is likely in the thousands.

"She's the mom I never had," was a classic line.

Barb was an enigma—a spitfire redhead with an infectious laugh, cleancut bob, and wire-rimmed glasses. She was a special education teacher for an elementary school before she got into the furniture world. Married and divorced from an alcoholic, she raised three children, got remarried, and ended up going into sales.

Her battle back from stage 4 cancer was a defining moment in her life. She ended up living 30+ years past her diagnosis. Barb's favorite saying was, "It's not about waiting for the storm to pass, but rather learning to dance in the rain."

In her career, Barb quickly rose in the ranks and became part-owner of Pivot Interiors. After working side-by-side for years, she finally corralled me into joining as her VP of Sales in San Francisco.

Barb saw my talent and ambition, and how much I cared about everything I did. She always said she saw herself in me, which may just be the best compliment in the world.

I soon became Barb's protégé.

"You're coming with me to Monterey this weekend!"

Together, we'd work our tails off during the week and entertain all weekend—only to do it all over again. It was like Auburn had been a training camp for success in the business world.

Despite having access to every technology at our fingertips, Barb's go-to communication was the sticky note. After any meeting, you could expect to walk away with a stack of colorful squares that she'd written your action items on.

It was the dawn of the Second Tech Boom when apps like Uber, Square, and Airbnb were born. Anyone you can imagine, any company you can imagine, Barb knew them all. She ended up landing contract after contract.

Barb was equal parts life of the party and Steady Eddie. She was the most positive person you'd ever meet, always there for you with her classic active listening and words of wisdom.

Barb was magic.

When she died unexpectedly in 2022, it felt like the entire corporate real estate industry in the Bay Area went into shock. We'd lost our heartbeat.

Her passing was a wake-up call for me. I realized that the life I was living wasn't the one I could be living.

*How can I make a bigger impact?* The question rang over and over in my head. That's when I decided I wanted to lead leaders on a global scale.

As I continue to grow my consultancy, my guiding principle will always be: What Would Barb Do?

*The Expert Generalist Lesson #27*
## LIVE A GREAT STORY

Life isn't about keeping score—it's about the impact we have on others. When people think of you, do they smile? How we treat friends, strangers, and the stories we leave behind shape our legacy. Barb inspired the tagline for my company, a vision that I hope we can all step into: Live a Great Story. Barb sure did.

*Cheers to Barbara Carlyle*

# CHAPTER TWENTY-EIGHT

"WE'RE ONE, BUT WE'RE NOT THE SAME
WE GET TO CARRY EACH OTHER."

-ONE BY U2

# UNCLE ANDY & AUNT MO

Y ou need to meet Andy."
I had just shown my friend my list of pre-date qualifications—an unofficial 'Do not pass go if you can't check the box.'

"Is he your only single friend?" I laughed back. It had become a running joke to set Mo up with any ol' Joe Schmo.

The first time Andy and I ever communicated was in a group text about football. Auburn had beat Oregon in the National Championship Game (War Eagle!). He sent me a separate text and we started a fun back-and-forth.

Our friend crew set up a coastal weekend in Gearhart, Oregon but I soon found out, it was pretty much couples only.

This could get awkward. All good, I was ready with an escape hatch: I booked a hotel room, got my own rental car, and had an excuse in my back pocket if I needed to leave in a hurry.

Andy thought we should talk on the phone before we met up with the group. During each call, he was super attentive. He listened. He asked interesting questions. He loved music and nature. I pretty much knew before I ever met him that Andy was a keeper.

"I really like you," he kept saying that first night.

"I really like you too."

Andy stood out. You could just tell he was a Boy Scout, a truly good person to the core.

*I'm gonna be open*, I decided. Worst case, he could be a new friend, maybe even a travel buddy since we had so much in common.

Our first trip was (no surprise) a road trip. We drove from Christmas in Seattle to seeing Oregon play in the Rose Bowl in Los Angeles. Since then, we've clocked tens of thousands of miles together.

Very early on, we went to Spain, Ireland, Italy, and all over the U.S.

One time, at a hotel in Santa Barbara, someone was trying to help me with my bags.

"I'm good," I said. "I'm waiting for my travel partner."

"Travel partner?" Andy's smile came around the corner.

"Or what do you want to call it?"

From there, he moved on to my "boy-friendly." In my forties, he was my second relationship ever.

Around that time, my neurotic sleepwalking stopped. Ever since I was little, I had these intense Frankenstein episodes at night. I would somehow get a chair, unlock all the padlocks my mom had installed, and end up outside.

During the 17 year marriage, I would walk around like a zombie, checking the locks of every house we lived in.

"Did you lock the door? Did you lock the door?"

For my entire life, I never felt safe.

With Andy, my nervous system knew. Finally, I didn't need to be the protector anymore.

It was a classic, "When you know, you know."

Not only do we both like to laugh and make jokes, but we don't like to fight. We both have the self-awareness to know that when we screw up, we say we're sorry. We're both givers, too.

Neither of us had kids, and after we met our nieces and nephews, we jokingly started calling one another Aunt & Uncle.

After over a decade together, the only thing we need from each other is each other.

*The Expert Generalist Lesson #28*
## SOMETIMES YOU JUST HAVE TO WAIT

A true partnership is like sweet tea steeping in the sun; it takes time to develop the full flavor. In business and in life, relationships thrive on aligned values, mutual respect, and clear communication. It's about clean agreements, staying on the same page, and building a foundation of trust. Good things really do come to those who wait.

In my case, it was just a quick 40 years.

# CHAPTER TWENTY NINE

**THEY GREW UP** WASHING THEIR CLOTHES & BATHING IN A CREEK **IN RURAL ALABAMA.**

# TAKE IT EASY

W hen are you going to get me out of here?" my mom asks these days, every time I see her.

Her question pulls me back to that memory when I was three years old, asking her the same from that bathroom stall. How the tables have turned.

My mom's life was hard. Born into extreme poverty during the aftermath of the Great Depression, she was the child of violent, alcoholic parents—left mostly to fend for herself, along with four siblings. They grew up washing their clothes and bathing in a creek in rural Alabama. Though she tried to give us a better life, she didn't have the education, support, or tools to do so.

During the three decades she was with her deadbeat husband, she would rent one hotel room after another, trying to unsuccessfully hide from the abuse. He was living in the only home she'd known since she'd had us and she didn't know how to get out.

Even as her dementia worsened, my mom knew who she could count on.

"I'm not doing anything until Monique gets here," she would say, when others tried to get into her bank account.

"Cain't I just come live with you?" she would ask me all the time.

Jesus, her Lord and Savior, never did step in, despite my mom's unwavering faith. She'd still be sitting in her trailer praying to win the Publishers Clearing House if we hadn't concocted a great escape.

"Monique's in town," my older brother told her husband, drunk on the couch like any other night. "We're going to dinner. Be back soon."

We picked my mom up with nothing but a purse and the clothes on her back. That was the last time she would ever see Alabama.

Off to Walmart for a new wardrobe and after a few stopovers down South due to COVID-19, she began a new life in Oregon, down the road from me.

"She's the happiest person that's ever lived here," the nurses at her memory care facility often say.

Despite the tragedy of my mom's life, she's always smiling.

Life gave her every reason to give up and, still, she trained herself to be kind and have grace. Even with advanced Alzheimer's, she retained this way of being even after she lost her mental and physical capacities.

Some people with dementia turn into Godzilla. But not my mom. The picture of resilience in action, she conditioned herself to smile through anything.

TAKE IT EASY, TAKE IT EASY

DON'T LET THE SOUND OF YOUR OWN WHEELS MAKE YOU CRAZY

COME ON, BABY, DON'T SAY MAYBE

I GOTTA KNOW IF YOUR SWEET LOVE IS GONNA SAVE ME

-TAKE IT EASY BY THE EAGLES

**THE PICTURE OF** RESILIENCE **IN ACTION, SHE CONDITIONED HERSELF TO** SMILE THROUGH ANYTHING.

That's my wish for all of us: to do better and be better, and to take it easy on each other and ourselves.

My mom didn't provide us a home to go home to. She always needed help—from beginning to end. She did the best she could with what she had. Now, as her official guardian and secondary caregiver, it's my turn.

"How's your mom?" my friends and loved ones ask.

Someone's wiping her ass, feeding her three meals a day, changing her clothes, and laying her down in bed. I can guarantee you that, for the first time, she's living her best life.

*The Expert Generalist Lesson #29*
## SMILE OFTEN

Make it a choice. Our expressions trigger emotions, which impact our behavior—ultimately shaping our reality. There's even science behind it. The Facial Feedback Hypothesis suggests that the act of smiling or frowning influences brain waves.

When smiling becomes the default mode, we create a world worth smiling about.

# CHAPTER THIRTY

THERE ARE TWO
WAYS TO GET
DOWNTOWN
FROM MY HOUSE
NOWADAYS:
**A PAVED ROAD
AND A DIRT
ROAD. CAN YOU
GUESS WHICH
ONE I TAKE?**

# REWILDIN'

I remember being a little kid and asking my mom, "Why are you making us live this way?"

She'd planted us on a dirt road, on a free piece of land where she could park a trailer and barely survive. I saw it as poverty. At the same time, it was living off the land, figuring it out, and learning the power of hard work. It was self-sufficiency, skill-building, networking, taking risks, and hustling.

Turns out, these are all the best life and leadership lessons on the planet. Ones that you can only learn by doing. I worry that critical thinking is lost today. Growing up in the pre-Internet era, if I were driving around lost, I had no choice but to pull over and ask for directions, or get creative.

Once I left that trailer, it was time to cash in on my hard-earned lessons and design the future I wanted to live.

In my junior year of college, I made my first big rendering in design school. I drew something right out of an architecture and interiors magazine: a modern loft with tall windows, structural beams, wood floors, a large bookshelf, and abstract art—all anchored by classic furniture. This house was on the West Coast and I honored this vision by including a Totem Pole. No one else in the class had that element.

Little did I know, I had designed a vision board for my future.

When Andy and I stepped into our house for the first time, I felt a sense of déjà vu. Transported right to my drawing-come-to-life in Bend, Oregon. The clean lines, loft ceilings, and high beams were all there. Even the wood stove chimney mirrored the Totem Pole.

We knew right away this was home.

My upbringing might seem like a sad story to some, but it's been a gift to me. Early on, I learned that my inner strength and determination were some of the few things I could control. This lesson was on repeat, like a record skipping over and over again.

For years, I ran from simplicity. I chased city lights, big opportunities, and a polished version of success I thought I wanted. I was the first one in the office at 6am, determined to be seen as the hardest worker in the room.

That drive, that moxy—it's what got me here. But it's also what weighed me down. At some point, I realized I wasn't chasing what I truly wanted; I was running from what I thought I didn't.

Turns out, what we run from often becomes what we're drawn back to.

My concept of Rewilding is a reclamation not just of the land, but of myself. Rewilding has been about returning to what I've always known. Stripping away the noise, complications, and expectations to find something real and rooted.

I designed a life for myself: house, place, style, and partner included. This was not handed to me. I have it because I envisioned it and built it, piece by piece.

Nature always calls me back. Pine trees, dirt roads, and quiet sunrises feel like home wherever I go, like the land whispering, "You've been here before." Moving to Central Oregon, was coming home to myself—sunny skies, woodsy adventure out the door, plenty of (actual) lakes, and letting the rhythm of nature remind me who I am. One hike at a time.

There are two ways to get downtown from my house nowadays: a paved road and a dirt road. Can you guess which one I take?

*The Expert Generalist Lesson #30*
## REMEMBER WHERE YOU COME FROM

Just as nature flourishes when it's allowed to return to its natural state, so do you when you reconnect with the things that shaped you. By embracing your roots, you allow yourself to grow in a way that's authentic and true to who you were always meant to be.

# On to the Next Chapter

It's funny how life comes full circle.

The path that got me here wasn't simple. My stepping stones were education, building life-long relationships, taking risks, and asking for feedback. Success requires mental fortitude, self-discipline, and the ability to separate truth from make-believe.

Life isn't a paved interstate with clear signs and a rest stop every 20 miles. It's more like a dirt road in Alabama: bumpy, unpredictable, occasionally littered with oddball characters shouting into bullhorns, and always full of potential if you look for the forest through the trees.

Becoming an Expert Generalist means embracing life as a perpetual student. It involves drawing lessons from every facet of every experience.

Generalistists aren't here to memorize the map; we're here to draw it. We're here to step into spaces where no one's sure what to do next and say, "I've never done this before, but let's give it a shot." We're here to stand tall, make a new plan, and occasionally shout back at the Devil—whether it shows up as a challenge at work, a personal struggle, or a person.

One thing is clear: expertise isn't just mastering one thing—it's embracing the mess of it all. It's about being able to build a home wherever you are, nurture and grow relationships, climb career ladders, and speak up for yourself and others. It's about taking every detour, pothole, and 'wrong' turn and turning them into a lesson—or at least a story for later.

So, as you close this book, I leave you with this: embrace your challenges (aka gifts), your winding path, and your knack for turning chaos into a life you want to live out loud everyday. Celebrate the moments when you didn't have it all figured out but figured it out anyway. And never forget that even on the roughest roads, there's always room for good trouble, a little laughter, and a whole lot of grit.

**So, Here's the Deal, Y'all...**

**Be a sponge.** Absorb everything life has to offer.

**Be purposeful.** Don't just move through life; make your mark with intention.

**Be a mentor.** Lift others up. Share your wisdom. Be someone's guiding light.

**Be MAGIC in the lives of others.** Sometimes, the smallest spark can ignite the brightest flame for someone else.

And above all: **BE YOURSELF.** Your truly, wonderfully, one-of-a-kind authentic self. No one else on this planet has what you have to offer. Your story, your voice, your impact—that's your greatest gift to the world.

The unpaved road isn't easy, but it's yours. Walk it, run it, stumble on it—just don't forget to keep going. And maybe, you'll inspire someone else to do the same.

Now go. **Be BOLD ... Be YOU**.

"SHE SAID:
'FREE YOURSELF
TO BE YOURSELF

IF ONLY YOU COULD
SEE YOURSELF

FREE YOURSELF,
TO BE YOURSELF

**IF ONLY YOU
COULD SEE'"**

-IRIS BY U2

# THANK YOU!
# THANK YOU!
# THANK YOU!

**Quinn Rose:** What began with your keen eye as a copyeditor evolved into a collaboration that elevated this book to something better than I could have imagined. Your remarkable ability to extract the heart of a narrative, challenge ideas, and shape them into something meaningful made the difference.

To the incredibly talented **Brandy Martin:** the creative force behind this book's design and illustration. Your artistry brought these pages to life, capturing the essence of my story in ways words alone could not. Beyond this book, you are the vision behind all things design for my brand. I'm beyond grateful for your magic.

Endless gratitude to **Alex Jordan** for your sharp eye, speed, and resourcefulness in bringing this book design to the finish line with us. Your talent and dedication were invaluable in making this vision a reality!

To my creative team in Alabama: **Ashley Kicklighter**, editorial photographing genius, and **Kirby Cox**, stylist extraordinaire. Can I get

an AMEN to this all-lady team of baddies? **My Mom, Emily Loraine Wright:** Mom gave me life and the foundation to make a positive impact. Her resilience and love are the roots of

everything I've become. She deserved better.
**My Granddaddy Louis:** For my first experience of love without condition and all the Nutter Butters a seven-year-old could want.

**My Alabama Family:** Uncle Beanie, Jerry, and Ray (all deceased); my Aunts, Janet and Dian; my cousins Mary Royal (aka Sister) and Trey Talton, Mark and Carolyn Stubbs, Christy

Guidry, Casey Royal and Cheyenne Talton.
**My Siblings:** Serge, Melissa, and Christopher; and Lauren Lecomte (deceased): I wish I could have

shown you a brighter world.

**Tootie's Family:** My brother-in-law, Mark; my

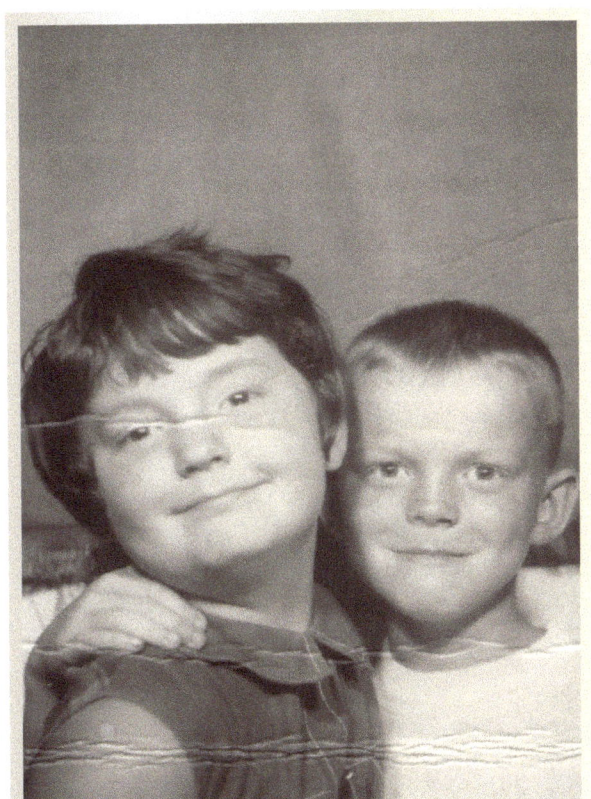

nephews Ethan and Isaac; and my niece Adelaide.

**To the incredible program directors at the Prattville YMCA:** Otis Reeves, John Manolakis, and Keith Cantrell—you lived the organization's core values of caring, honesty, respect, and responsibility in everything you do.

**To My YMCA Family:** Kelli, Nikki, Andy, Rob, Larry, Britney, Leigh Ann, Leslie, Stacy, James, Jody, Amy, and Abbie.

**Shannon DeLoach (my BFF, in loving memory):** I wish you were still here to share in all the mischief and the joy. You are missed and

were so loved. The truest friend in every since of the word.

**My Old Prattville Friends:** Jennifer MacNiven (bestie and my photographer for life), Bob and Kathleen Champion, Kristy Cone Myers, Bobby Bush, and Michael Lolley.

**My Alaska homesteaders:** David, Dianne, Cyndie Bridges, and Laurie Smith—you will always be a part of one of my most incredible stories.

**Auburn University Professors, Roommates and Classmates:** Dr. Dotty Cavender, Susan Hawk, Rob Smith (one of the first people I met in AU), Mike Mosquito, Corry Mansell, Selena Lee, Veronique Copeland, Adrienne Williams, Amanda Moreau, Molly Burton, Jack Slaughter + the entire Saugahatchee Crew, Robin Adams, Dr. Mary Ann Potter, Dr. June Henton (in memory), Melanie Rainwater, Nancy Cox and the entire Cox family (Big Daddy and Queen), Katrina Huston, Karen Royal, Karen Ross, Mike Quick, Chris Vasallo (my road trip partner out West), Mike McClinton, The Auburn Swimming & Diving Team 1992-1996, AU Pike House, Sigma Chi House, and *Rebecca Dowdy (my first book supporter!)*.

**The Non-Icy Seattle Posse:** Kyle Kirby for being up for a cross-country move at the drop of a hat, Teresa Terry (my ride or die at any hour), Michelle Vernarelli, Kira Cowan, Kelly Coller & Tony Secolo, Tirzah Griffin, Terri Lundberg, Chad & Nate Jackson, Greg Cobb, Todd Johnson & Doug McKenzie, Lisa Detweiler, Karen Holm, Cheryl Bobson,

Quinton Hooks, and Marjorie Chang.

**My Work Families...**

**Sechrist Design Associates:** Melinda and Mike Sechrist, Debbie (in memory), Stephanie, and Gordon.

**BINW:** Carolyn Barnes (in remembrance), we miss you every day; Angie Moawad, Ann Conklin, Karen Kramer (my friend and confidante), Sean O'Brien, Rich Lacher, Dave and Florence Covey, Robert Barnes, Sunny Jim and all of the amazing women at BINW.

**Knoll:** Everyone from the dot-bomb era, Kathleen Neary (my soul sister), John Norfolk, Vicki Rova-Mueller, David Dorn (in memory), Rich Cummings, Mike Benigno, Tony Bello (fondly remembered), Allison Ferraro, Susie Hansen, Kara Ugarte, Debbie Williams, Peg Conley, Gina Harper, and Liz Follis (my friend for life).

**Herman Miller:** Jerry Koster, Michael Tilbrooke, Mike Doody, Sheryl Smith (fondly remembered), PJ Anderson (my first SF roomie and forever mentor), Carie Mueller, Fae Urban, Cecilia Lyra, Alex Yakutis, Carla Dore, Lorraine Cassis, Carol Austin, and the kick-ass Strategic Accounts Group in the 2000s (man, were we lucky).

**My Denver Ladies:** Kelly Donovan, Kristen Weede Cummings, Hillary Ellis, Jennifer

Harding, Erin Niehus, Twilla Case, Casey Keasler, Jenny Massey, and Kristen Cornella. **Dave McElhany:** the best thing that came from my marriage. You had a true giver's heart, and I am so sorry you were surrounded by vampires. RIP.

**Pivot Interiors:** Barbara Carlyle (in loving memory), Ken Baugh, Harvey Vander Baan, Patrick Donlon, Dennis Oliver, Cathy Nakasora, Jesse Michael (in remembrance), Susan Spielman, LuAnn Kane, Paola Sprenzel, Amy Hanlon, Mica Guitron, Tasnim Punjabi, Amy Storek,

and so many more...

**Shaw:** Derek Wallace, Pam Randles, Daniel Collins, Oriana Reich, John Cantrell, Steve Brownlee, Kelly Fain, Karolina Graves, Chelsie St. James, along with so many others.

**Hightower:** The Kathyrn Lamb (my bestie and roomie), Natalie Hartkopf, Wendy Nichols, Kent Lusk, Mark Beard, Whitney Joly, Kristen Decker, Erin Greig, and Adam Merkl, as well as all the fantastic men and women at Hightower (yes, men work there too!) Also to my fabulous international partners in crime, Lars,

Christian, Marika and Jonas as well as all of the talented rep groups across North America. **ALL of my San Francisco, Portland and Bend Friends:** PJ Anderson and Bruce Bean, SMDC, Cliff and Andrea Berry, Andrea and Tom Tobias, Gary and Karen Wells, Jill Arias and Brett Rolfe, Jeff and Heather Fini, Ellen and Rish Spurlock, Jenn Vannetta, Colleen Kellog, Adrienne Wannamaker. and everyone else. There are too many to count.

**And the 1,000s of amazing friends and mentors throughout this journey:** You are all a part of my story and have impacted my life for the better. Thank you all, all y'all.

**Cheers to the Snakes:** You know who you are. I thank you for changing my life trajectory in the opposite direction.

**And lastly, my VIPs for life…**

**Melissa "Tootie" Harmon:** My sister, cheerleader, and OG bestie. I mean, you really have to like each other to be as close as we are after sharing a bed for 16 years. And thank you for being Chief Optimist at Monique Lecomte, Elevating Others!

**Andy Wiedemann:** (last but not least) my faithful, trusting, kind, and caring life partner. My favorite travel buddy and concert +1. What would I do without you? You have shown me that having a ***good person*** in your life can exist in more than words.

# SOUTHERN
## SAYIN'S

## ALL Y'ALL
Every single one of you.

## ALL HAT AND NO CATTLE
Someone who talks big but doesn't deliver or have substance.

## AW LAWD OR OH LORT
An expression of surprise or disbelief, similar to 'Oh Lord.'

## BAT SHIT CRAZY
Extremely irrational.

## BIRD DOG
A term for someone who helps find or secure something, often in a business or deal-making context.

## BLESS YER HEART
This can be genuine sympathy, or a sarcastic way to say someone is clueless.

## BOONDOCKS
A remote or rural area far from the city.

## CATTY-CORNER OR KITTY-CORNER
Adjacent to.

## CAIN'T NEVER COULD
You can't succeed if you don't try; often used to encourage effort.

## CAN'T CARRY A TUNE IN A BUCKET
Terrible at singing.

## CATAWAMPUS
*kat-uh-wom-puhs*
*adjective*
Askew, crooked, or not straight.

## CLUE SHACK
Someone who is clueless or doesn't understand what's happening.

## COME TO JESUS MEETING
A serious conversation or moment of truth.

## DRUNK AS COOTER BROWN

Extremely drunk. Cooter Brown is a legendary figure known for being perpetually intoxicated.

## FIRE AND BRIMSTONE

A preaching style that uses vivid, terrifying imagery of divine punishment and Hell to warn about the consequences of sin.

## FIXIN' TO

Means getting ready to do something, while "fixings" refers to side dishes, typically with a meal.

## FULL AS A BLUE TICK

Full, often after overeating.

## FUNNY AS ALL GET OUT

Hilarious.

## GET 'ER DONE

A call to complete a task or get something done.

## GIMME SOME SUGAR

A request for affection, usually meaning a kiss.

## HANKERIN'

A strong desire or craving.

## HEAVENS TO BETSY

Similar to *"Oh my goodness!"* or *"Well, I'll be!"*

## HIGH COTTON

Doing well, especially financially.

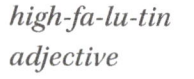

## HIGHFALUTIN

*high-fa-lu-tin*
*adjective*
Fancy, pretentious, or superior.

## HONKY TONK

A cheap or disreputable bar, club, or dance hall, typically where country music is played.

## HOTTER THAN A WHORE IN CHURCH

Feeling very uncomfortable, nervous, or out of place in a situation, typically due to guilt or shame.

## I'LL BE A MONKEY'S UNCLE
An expression of surprise or disbelief.

## IF THE CREEK DOESN'T RISE
Nothing goes wrong or unexpected happens.

## LIKE WHITE ON RICE
Very close or inseparable.

## LORDY LORDY
An expression of exasperation or surprise.

## MADDER THAN A WET HEN
Very angry.

## OVER YONDER
A vague direction, meaning "over there" somewhere far.

## PIDDLIN'
*pid-l-in*

*verb*

To waste time doing trivial tasks or things of little importance.

## SLAP OUT
Completely out of. Also the name of a town in Alabama.

## SHO NUFF
Sure enough.

## USED TO COULD
Something one used to be able to do but can't anymore.

## WHAT IN TARNATION!?
An expression of confusion or disbelief.

## WORKIN' MY TAIL OFF
Working very hard.

## WORN SLAP OUT
Exhausted or completely worn out.

## Y'ALL AIN'T RIGHT
Playfully accusing someone of being strange or funny in an endearing way.

## Y'ALL NEED JESUS
A colloquial phrase used humorously, seriously, or ironically to comment on someone's behavior or actions.

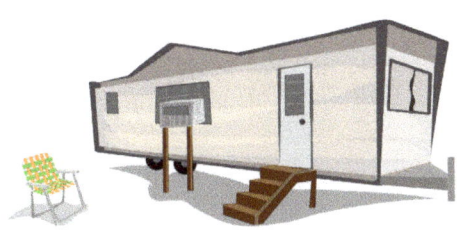

MONIQUE LECOMTE is a keynote speaker, leadership expert, and facilitator with a career spanning 20+ years in global business for iconic brands– Herman Miller, Knoll, and Hightower. Growing up in rural Alabama, she learned resilience and adaptability—skills that shaped her journey from small-town life to the boardroom. A recognized **Expert Generalist**, she has built high-performing teams, driven cultural change, and helped organizations thrive by balancing innovation with a human connection.

A certified *Leadership Challenge*® facilitator and *Leadership Practices Inventory* coach, Monique works with executives and teams to redefine leadership for the modern world.

Monique lives in beautiful Bend, Oregon, with her partner, Andrew, where she enjoys hiking, traveling and stargazing when she is not perfecting her biscuit recipe.

🌐 MONIQUELECOMTE.COM 📷 MONIQUELECOMTE_ELEVATINGOTHERS

www.ingramcontent.com/pod-product-compliance
Lightning Source LLC
Chambersburg PA
CBHW041535120626
46551CB00019B/2713